A Manager's Guide to ISO22301

A practical guide to developing and implementing a business continuity management system

A Manager's Guide to ISO22301

A practical guide to developing and implementing a business continuity management system

TONY DREWITT

IT Governance Publishing

Every possible effort has been made to ensure that the information contained in this book is accurate at the time of going to press, and the publishers and the author cannot accept responsibility for any errors or omissions, however caused. Any opinions expressed in this book are those of the author, not the publisher. Websites identified are for reference only, not endorsement, and any website visits are at the reader's own risk. No responsibility for loss or damage occasioned to any person acting, or refraining from action, as a result of the material in this publication can be accepted by the publisher or the author.

IT Governance Publishing
IT Governance Limited
Unit 3, Clive Court
Bartholomew's Walk
Cambridgeshire Business Park
Ely
Cambridgeshire
CB7 4EA
United Kingdom

www.itgovernance.co.uk

First published in the United Kingdom in 2013
by IT Governance Publishing

ISBN 978-1-84928-467-7

ABOUT THE AUTHOR

Tony Drewitt is a business continuity practitioner and a professional member of the Business Continuity Institute (BCI). He has been a practising consultant in the field of operational risk management and business continuity management (BCM) since 2001, working with a wide range of small, medium and large organisations, to develop BCM policies, strategies and plans.

Tony started his career as a mechanical engineer in industry, and has held a range of posts in sales and marketing, general management and management consulting. He was one of the first practitioners to achieve certification under BS25999 (predecessor to ISO22301) for a client in 2008, and is currently working with a number of clients on developing management systems for both standards.

Tony is the author of the already successful ITG publications *BS25999: A Pocket Guide*, *A Manager's Guide to BS25999* and *Everything You Want to Know about Business Continuity*.

CONTENTS

Contents

Contents

INTRODUCTION

BS25999-2, the predecessor to ISO22301, was first published in November 2007, yet, after five years, business continuity continues to be something of a mystery to a great many people involved in running organisations today. The majority are not actually required, either by law or by anybody else, to demonstrate any form of business continuity arrangements, so business continuity management (BCM) has not, until recently, been seen as a priority for these organisations. The global economic recession has also reduced the emphasis, placed by many, upon operational risk management and supplier assurance.

Yet the world continues to change. There is an apparent growth in the number of threats to the ability of organisations to continue with their business activities. This is coupled with increasingly sophisticated approaches to corporate governance, risk management, and corporate and social responsibility. These factors fuel the growing need for organisations to demonstrate, and provide assurance that, should some interruptive incident occur, they have done everything reasonable to minimise disruption to the continued supply of products or services in which they are engaged.

The increasing levels of competition, not only in the UK and Europe, but from around the globe, mean that, in the commercial world, letting down customers as a result of what would have previously been seen as 'not your fault', carries increasingly higher penalties, as business can often be lost for good.

Before the introduction of BS25999, it was arguably not worthwhile for organisations to invest in a BCM programme, and whilst take up of this standard is encouraging, both in the UK and around the world, it is likely that many more organisations have held back in anticipation of what they may see as the 'ultimate', an international standard.

Now that this has arrived, it still remains for each national standards body to decide upon its formal introduction for certification purposes, and in the UK, and elsewhere, where BS25999 and other national standards are used, these bodies must decide upon the transition from one standard to the next.

It is likely to take at least 12 months for most organisations to develop and implement a worthwhile BCM system; with today's competitive pressures, the only really sensible path is to have implemented such a system before it is formally demanded by customers, regulators, or even the law. As with international standards in many other management disciplines, ISO22301 will very soon become the only benchmark by which others can judge that an organisation's BCM arrangements are fit for purpose.

Please note that, since the printed version of this book is produced in black and white, patterns have been used here to represent red, amber and green, colours which are widely employed in business continuity management to indicate levels of criticality.

The patterns in use are:

Red ▦ **Amber** ▦ **Green** ▤

CHAPTER 1: INTRODUCING BUSINESS CONTINUITY MANAGEMENT

What is business continuity management?

Business continuity management (BCM), or business continuity (BC) as it is more commonly named, is essentially a form of risk management that deals with the risk of business activities, or processes, being interrupted by external factors, as distinct from business or commercial risks, such as, for example, the loss of a supplier or foreign exchange losses.

All organisations conduct risk management in connection with many, or even all, of their activities; however, this is often done intuitively and is unlikely to cover all aspects of the organisation's operations.

Organisations of all types carry a variety of risks, both operational and strategic.

Figure 1 shows some examples of business interruption and continuity risks in the context of the overall risk spectrum.

Later in this book, we will look at the scope of business continuity, and how certain risks, or scenarios, may fall within, or outside that scope, depending upon the individual organisation's policy.

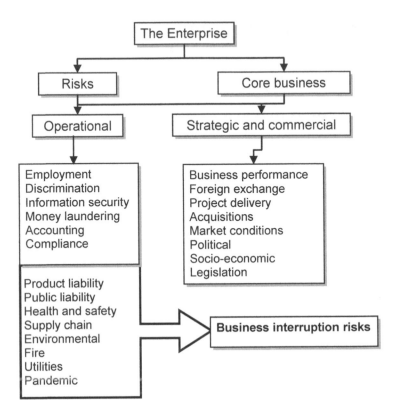

Figure 1: Business interruption and continuity risks

Evolution

Business continuity management really evolved from the older discipline of Information Technology Disaster Recovery (ITDR), during a time when systematic approaches to business management were becoming increasingly popular. This coincided, to some extent, with the growth of corporate governance standards which included a significant focus upon the management of risk.

During the late 1970s and 1980s, as computers were introduced to many business processes, their relative unreliability, and the potential to lose all of the organisation's critical information in one go, revealed the need for methods of backing up and retrieving data, and the computer systems themselves.

The ITDR industry has, since the late 1970s, become very well established, and it is now unthinkable for almost any organisation to have no data or hardware back-up and recovery arrangements.

As modes of doing business expanded rapidly during the 1980s and 1990s, and as previously unthinkable incidents started to have a real impact on businesses and other organisations, the discipline of 'business continuity' evolved as a way of minimising the impact of any operational interruption that might occur.

The new business of corporate governance also began making it necessary for boards to ensure that risk control measures generally were much more systematic. They needed to be commensurate with the risks they addressed, and to be documented so that the organisation's preparedness could be properly audited and assessed, and so that, in the event of a real incident, it could be shown that the organisation had taken appropriate steps to minimise impact and protect the interests of its stakeholders.

The growth of the business continuity industry was arguably led by the financial services sector (particularly the larger banking institutions) which is regulated by the Financial Services Authority (FSA) in the United Kingdom, the Securities Exchange Commission (SEC) in the United States, and by similar regulatory bodies in the vast majority of developed countries around the world. Whilst the UK's Financial Services Act itself does not stipulate a requirement for regulated firms to 'do' business continuity management, the FSA's Business Continuity Management Practice Guide makes it clear to those firms that they are expected to have a business continuity management system based upon good practice principles.

In the US, the Sarbanes-Oxley Act, contrary to the claims of some practitioners, again does not expressly require firms to have BCM arrangements in place, and here, as in many other similar pieces of legislation around the world, there is likely to be some form of implicit requirement to manage and control operational risks, which must include operational interruptions.

As one would expect, the reliance of many firms within the financial services sector on large information systems operating on very short time scales, dealing with banking transactions and the like, has meant that they had to ensure a high level of ITDR capability. It therefore became a natural extension of this management discipline to put similar arrangements in place for all other operational aspects of the business.

The Business Continuity Institute (BCI) was established in 1994 by a number of business continuity practitioners, many of whom were IT professionals working in the financial services sector. Also during the 1990s, the British Standards Institution (BSI) published a document called *Publicly Available Specification 56* (PAS56), which attempted to set out a methodical approach to business continuity.

PAS56 was superseded by BS25999 in 2007, but it was, for some time, the only standard guide to business continuity management.

These developments have all contributed to the growth of a discernible business continuity industry which comprises a wide variety of in-house practitioners, contingency resource providers, software tool developers and out-sourced professional service providers, helping many organisations to rapidly establish a fit-for-purpose system.

The differences between PAS56 and BS25999 were very significant, and the latter did a good job of establishing a sensible framework for how organisations might go about 'systemising' their arrangements for operational resilience and responding to incidents.

The differences between BS25999 and ISO22301 are arguably less significant; many of the changes are more to do with fitting the ISO standard format, but there are also some which simplify the requirements, are more logical, and remove some of the jargon that is not always seen as helpful.

Most significantly, any organisation that is already developing other management systems, or has them in place, should find that a business continuity management system developed under ISO22301 is much easier to integrate with others.

The business continuity management system (BCMS)

Business continuity is really a contingent discipline that is only required in the event of an interruption. It could be likened to a car driver having a subscription to a vehicle breakdown assistance service. If that driver did not know how to contact the service, or did not know under which circumstances the service could be invoked, then its value would be very much reduced.

Similarly, with business continuity, the organisation that has experienced an interruption may need to invoke alternative resources to enable it to resume its operational activities. If it is to achieve this, the right information and the right resources must be available.

Here, the distinction between business continuity (BC) and disaster recovery (DR) is important. The principal instrument of BC is the BC plan (BCP); the tool that guides the organisation's management in responding to, and recovering from, an interruption, in the best possible way. However, the BCP will only be effective if the DR resources that it cites are actually available, and provide the functions and capacity that the plan expects.

Good practice in business continuity management today is about being able to deal with a wide range of interruption scenarios, having contingency resources that are commensurate with the business processes they support, having effective documented plans that will work because they are 'owned' by the organisation and kept up to date, and having a capable team of people who can lead the organisation's response and recovery.

This good practice can be delivered by a systematic approach that is enshrined within *ISO22301:2012 Societal security – Business continuity management systems – Requirements.*

This book provides practical, detailed guidance on all the steps necessary for an organisation to develop, and implement, a business continuity management system that is capable of certification to this standard.

The relationship between business continuity and disaster recovery

In reality, the terms 'business continuity' and 'disaster recovery' are interchangeable. The result of doing disaster recovery properly is that the business (or other organisation) resumes what it was doing before being interrupted – in other words, that it continues. 'Business continuity' was introduced as a way of differentiating something that just restored computer systems and data, from something that restored business processes and entire organisations.

It is really just a matter of evolution that 'disaster recovery' has come to mean arrangements for replacing resources, whereas 'business continuity' has come to mean a broader, management discipline, including planning and DR, which should ensure the continued operation of an organisation following some interruption.

As previously mentioned, the ITDR industry is probably the most mature part of the BCM world, but IT or ICT (Information Communications Technology) is only part of the resource base for any organisation. *Chapter 4* of this book looks in some detail at what is referred to as 'BC strategy', that is, deciding how the operational resources upon which the organisation depends, will be both protected from threats, and replaced in the event they are disabled.

So, DR is really about all the organisation's operational resources, not just the IT or ICT systems, and this area is also frequently referred to as 'resilience'. That title, of course, implies that the resource in question will not fail in the first place.

An obvious example for explaining this terminology is the typical IT system in *Example 1*, below.

Example 1: Failover resilience

A company with a local area network (LAN) in its offices might invest in a 'failover' facility. This means that, should the server that provides the company's staff with applications and data fail, another server will, often automatically, take the place of the failed server, so that the staff can continue doing their jobs.

This is resilience of the IT applications (and their associated data), but it is provided by what is known as a DR service, which might also be employed in the event that the company's entire office building was destroyed.

Disaster recovery can, and often does, exist on its own. However, it is also an essential component in BCM, because it provides the necessary resources that enable business processes to be executed, when required. It should also be noted that DR does not, itself, include any proactive risk management, and, whilst the selection of DR arrangements is sometimes based upon a risk assessment, it is perhaps more often based upon an intuitive understanding of what resilience or contingencies are required.

Cause and effect

There are many reasons why an organisation's normal activities could be interrupted, and whilst cause, or threat, is an important part of risk assessment and the development of resilience, much of BCM is about effect. The impact of an activity being interrupted should be more or less the same, whether the interruption is caused by a fire, a terrorist act, global warming or pandemic flu.

This distinction actually makes the BCM practitioner's life a bit simpler, not least because many plans and response mechanisms can be 'universal', focusing on restoring only the interrupted activity.

That said, there is definitely a place for scenario-based plans, but, as we shall see, these, again, can encompass a range of causes or threats, so that the overall arrangements may be as simple as possible.

BCM policy

What is policy?

BCM policy is something that has escaped many organisations attempting to put a sensible BCM system in place, usually because there has been no clear idea of what such a policy should be.

The real purpose of having a BCM policy is to ensure consistency and objectivity in the way that different parts of an organisation are protected by the various measures that the BCMS involves. It can also help to optimise the resourcing of BCM by, for example, defining the scope of what parts of the organisation are to be covered by the protection of BCM, so that one, low value activity, does not receive more protection than another activity of higher value.

In some organisations the policy can be useful in securing collaboration. Not everybody wants to get involved in BCM straight away, and sometimes the existence of a policy – a statement of requirement from the Board – can help in getting people behind the project, and the work that needs to be done.

Policy can also be useful as a form of corporate assurance. When a legitimate, interested party, such as a customer, wants assuring that one of their suppliers won't let them down, a written policy can often be more useful than a verbal assurance, especially when the former is much more likely to be supported by real resilience arrangements.

These objectives should be met by a written policy document that includes, *inter alia*, the elements below.

- A statement of intent, purpose, objectives and any external compliance requirements for BCM; the policy statement.
- Scope – this may specify parts, or aspects of the organisation, that are to be included, or excluded, from the BCMS, such as:
  - Business units or divisions
  - Types of business process
  - Financial values
  - Geographic or other territories
  - Types of risk; physical, internal/external, strategic, financial, etc.
- Criteria for measuring and assessing impact, and the likelihood of threats materialising.
- Classification of risks, such as: acceptable, tolerable and intolerable.
- Rules for controlling (mitigating) and monitoring risks in different classifications, including timescales, where relevant.
- Assignment of responsibilities and parameters for developing, maintaining and testing the BCMS.
- A process for providing assurance to the Board or governing body, as to the adequacy of the controls in

place for business interruption, and other risks that fall within the scope of the policy, and the plans and resources that effectively constitute those controls.

It is likely to make sense for most organisations that the policy serves as both an internal document and an external one, available to legitimate scrutineers who need to be satisfied that the organisation's business-interruption and similar risks are adequately controlled; and that it has taken all reasonable steps to ensure its continued operation and survival in the event of an unforeseen interruptive incident of significant proportions.

Although most of the key elements in the policy are described in greater detail throughout this book, the items below should also be considered.

The policy statement

Every organisation will be 'doing' BCM for its own reasons. These should be included in the policy statement, in a way that will make sense to all its audiences. The commitment to developing, implementing and maintaining a BCMS is important in any organisation:

- For employees, because it gives them an additional level of confidence in their employer's resilience.
- For managers, because it provides a mandate to engage in activities that contribute to development and maintenance of the BCMS, and effectively to use the organisation's resources in so doing.
- For customers and clients, because it provides additional assurance as to the resilience of their supplier; an element in the due diligence process.

- For suppliers, because it provides greater confidence in the robustness of their markets, particularly where the organisation is a major customer to any supplier.

The policy statement is also a good place to set out the objectives – more specific and measurable targets that represent the key benefits for the organisation in developing a BCMS. In some cases, it may be appropriate to develop key performance indicators (KPIs) from these objectives, the achievement of which is likely to mean that the objectives are being met. As we'll see later, amongst these KPIs are likely to be the regular and comprehensive review and updating of the various components of the BCMS. An increasingly likely objective is certification under ISO22301.

For some organisations, there are formal and informal statutory and non-statutory compliance requirements in respect of BCM, and these should be referred to in the policy statement.

The sectors where statutory compliance requirements currently exist are financial services, the public sector, the law and listed companies.

It should be understood that while, for the most part, the requirement to maintain a full BCMS is implicit within these compliance arrangements, a BCMS provides arguably the best way to meet and exceed some of these requirements and expectations.

There is a greater variety of non-statutory compliance requirements for many organisations, principally in the supply chain. Just as customers and clients have required that their suppliers meet certain assurance and management systems requirements, such as Quality (ISO9000),

Information Security (ISO27001 and ISO27002) Environmental Management (ISO14001) and Human Resources (Investor in People), so BCM is rapidly becoming a mandatory requirement for many. This is clearly a key reason to develop a BCMS and, of course, there is no better way to provide assurance, and meet compliance requirements, than to achieve certification under ISO22301.

An example of a BCM policy which meets the requirements of ISO22301 is to be found in *Appendix 1*.

Use of the policy

Many organisations are quite accustomed to publishing some, or all, of their policies, both internally and externally, so dealing with the BCM policy should not prove difficult.

Essentially, the policy is both a commitment to doing things, and a mandate to execute the tasks necessary to doing those things; in this case, the development and maintenance of a BCMS. The policy should, therefore, not contain any sensitive or confidential information, so that it can be published widely. If it is useful for the policy to take into account sensitive information, such as financial figures, this can simply be referred to in the policy, it need not be stated in the body of the document.

Scope is a key area where policy can be used to support the organisation's competitiveness. Some organisations may have a BCMS, or even certification under ISO22301 covering only a part of the organisation, such as the head office functions. Sometimes, the operational part of the organisation, upon which its customers would probably most rely, may not be covered at all. So a supplier which has, or is developing, a BCMS for which the scope is its entire operation, should use that as a competitiveness tool in differentiating itself from other suppliers.

CHAPTER 2: OVERVIEW OF THE BCM PROCESS

This chapter provides an overview of the BCM process and an introduction to *Chapters 3* to *9* of this book.

Unlike its predecessor, ISO22301 doesn't include a 'model' for the BCM process – something the former called 'the BCM Lifecycle', which was, in fact, quite similar to the 'Plan-Do-Check-Act' (PDCA) cycle which does form part of the basis of the Standard.

Whilst the resulting BC plans, and the organisation's ability to prevent or withstand interruptive incidents should ultimately be the same, the mechanism by which an ISO22301 compliant management system delivers these is distinctly different from BS25999.

This book's predecessor looked at the rationale for executing all of the BCM lifecycle's six components, on the basis of the 'whole is greater than the sum of the parts'. However, the structure of ISO22301 is consistent with other ISO management system standards, and it is really self-evident that for a management system to be compliant, it really must meet all of the specification, not selected parts of it. It is also intuitively obvious that most of the operation of the system simply cannot be done unless the scoping, specification and planning elements are in place.

The key sections of ISO22301 are:

Section	Title	Main components
4	Context of the organisation	Establishing and documenting: • What the organisation does, and the potential impact of disruptions • Relationship with other policies and wider risk management • Contractual and other requirements • Who are the interested parties • Scope of the management system
5	Leadership	Establishing and documenting: • Leadership and commitment with respect to BCM • A BCM policy • Roles, responsibilities and authorities
6	Planning	Determining and documenting: • The risks and opportunities presented by the objectives and requirements • BC objectives and plans to achieve them • Minimum acceptable levels of output • Some form of project plan, with an evaluation mechanism

7	Support	Establishing a range of resources that underpin the BCMS, including:
		• A competence system
		• An awareness programme
		• A communications plan, to include both incident and non-incident situations
		• Documentation and its management
8	Operation	Planning and implementing processes that deliver:
		• Business impact analysis and risk assessment
		• Strategies
		• (Contingency) resources
		• Impact mitigation
		• Incident response structure and plans
		• Exercise and test arrangements
9	Performance evaluation	Determining and documenting arrangements for:
		• Monitoring, measurement, analysis and evaluation
		• Internal audit
		• Management review

Section	Title	Main components
10	Improvement	Establishing procedures for: • Non-conformance identification, reporting and consequence control • Corrective actions (system changes) • Continual improvement

Figure 2: Key sections of ISO22301

Context of the organisation

Understanding of the organisation and its context

There are some who see this section as unnecessary, however, it provides evidence that the system is based upon a proper consideration of how the organisation works, its priorities and objectives.

Essentially, the system should include documented information on the following:

- The organisation's activities, functions, services and/or products, and its relationships with other parties, including its supply chains.
- The potential impact that might arise from a major operational disruption.
- How the business continuity policy fits into the organisation's overall activities, its other risk management policies and activities, and any other policies (such as information security, environmental management or human resources).
- Risk appetite and risk criteria.
- Internal and external threats – the Standard describes these as 'the external and internal factors that create the uncertainty that gives rise to risk'.
- The defined purpose of the BCMS.

In a way, the Standard is asking for proof that you really need BCM, that you understand the benefits of having it, and that everything is based upon an identified level of risk, or impact, tolerance – the risk appetite.

Understanding the needs and expectations of interested parties

Another facet of the rationale for the BCMS is understanding the needs and expectations of 'interested parties'. Aside from the obvious interest of the organisation's owners, it does make a lot of sense to establish what other interested parties might require, or expect, when it comes to operational resilience and the risks of interruption.

Interested parties may include:

- Customers or clients
- Employees
- Shareholders
- Suppliers
- The local community
- Licensors
- Insurers
- Bankers.

In most cases, the most significant of these is likely to be customers or clients, as they are likely to be the most affected by an interruption to the provision of products or services, and therefore to inflict the greatest long-term impact by, for example, not renewing a contract.

Determining the scope of the business continuity management system

Scope, in the context of organisational resilience, is something of a double-edged sword. On the one hand it means that by defining a narrow scope, an organisation can secure certification under this, and many other, standards, but on the other hand, this would also mean that the organisation is not as well protected as it would otherwise be, and unwitting customers may be duped into thinking that their supplier must be as resilient as possible because they have a BCMS certified to ISO22301. The Standard allows the organisation to decide what its scope should be, and this may come in the form of:

* Products and/or services
* Regions, areas or territories
* Operating divisions or other organisational entities
* Sites, locations or individual buildings
* Departments or divisions within an individual site or operating unit.

The scope should ideally be based upon a rational assessment of the organisation, what it does, its customers, and the needs of other stakeholders. Whilst the Standard doesn't stipulate how this is arrived at, certification assessment will probably require some explanation.

Business continuity management system

ISO22301 is a management system standard; its rationale is that if the resilience and response capabilities are based upon an operating system, as opposed to just having a plan, for example, then those capabilities are likely to be as good as they can be. The requirement to have a management system therefore seems obvious, and it is arguably similar to what BS25999 referred to as programme management.

BS25999 made a point of requiring a programme management component, but didn't really explain what the actual requirements were. ISO22301 does an arguably better job by requiring, in section 5 (leadership), that:

'Top management shall demonstrate leadership and commitment with respect to the BCMS by (*inter alia*) ...

Ensuring that the resources needed for the business continuity management system are available, and;

Directing and supporting persons to contribute to the effectiveness of the BCMS'.

These two specific requirements, from clause 5.2 Management Commitment, suggest that there needs to be a visible programme, with the resources (including staff time) and corporate backing, to deliver a fit-for-purpose management system. To try to do this any other way would almost certainly be at odds with the way that any organisation works, and would simply be counter-intuitive.

The existence of a formal BCM programme usually gives it a much better foothold in the organisation; a visible presence and natural degree of importance that encourages the majority of people to treat it more seriously, and actually to do the tasks that have been assigned to them, or to make time for meetings and workshops.

A formal BCM programme also becomes a legitimate item for progress-reporting to the Board, or governing body of the organisation, on a regular basis, engaging the most senior managers and adding to momentum.

The existence of the management system and programme really go hand-in-hand; the programme provides the momentum, and the management system is a readily identifiable 'thing' that managers can develop, operate and own.

Leadership

Some organisations, or more usually departments, have tried to develop BCM arrangements without the genuine commitment and support of their board, or governing body. Often, this may be in response to a particular customer requirement, or perhaps compliance with some code that relates only to the department in question, or what it does. This may be possible in a small minority of cases, but the rationale behind both BS25999 and ISO22301 is that without genuine, demonstrable, commitment and support from the Board, BCM capabilities will simply not be as good, or effective, as they could be.

Policy

The BCM policy is where a number of faccts of commitment can be demonstrated. It is:

• A statement of corporate intent (to optimise the organisation's operational resilience).
• An executive mandate for managers to develop, and operate, the BCMS.
• A marketing asset; to promote the organisation amongst customers, investors, suppliers, potential employees and other stakeholders.
• A summary of BCM objectives and requirements.

The policy is, of course, a document that embodies the organisation's commitment and authority to optimise its resilience.

Roles, responsibilities and authorities

Another piece of reasonably, undeniable logic, is that if named individuals are not assigned both responsibility and accountability, to develop and maintain the system, and to act in the event of an incident, then the overall capability will be diminished. There are anecdotes of organisations that adopt the 'whoever gets there first' approach, and some that assign system maintenance responsibility to a team. However, experience shows that the best way to ensure things get done correctly, and on time, especially in a crisis, is to assign responsibility to named individuals, and to be clear about what each person's responsibilities, and authority to act, are.

Planning

This is, probably, the most widely-recognised aspect of BCM, and usually the part that gets done when all others do not. The plan is the collateral that the organisation's response team, if it has one, need to arrive at the best decisions in the event of an incident. However, the planning section of the Standard calls for a whole-range of documented information that logically underpins the BCP, and should make sure that it has the best chance of working as intended.

There should be some actions taken to 'address risks and opportunities'. Addressing risks is intuitively obvious; it is about the risks of operational interruption, and the actions are likely to include elements of the response part of the BCP, but may also include others in the risk assessment section. Actions to address opportunities may be less obvious, but may well include, for example, using BCM as a promotional and competitiveness tool, optimising expenditure on operational risk management controls, and integrating the BCMS with other management systems.

A clear statement of business continuity objectives is required, and this must be consistent with the BCM policy. The rationale is simple; if you don't have any BCM (related) objectives, then there is no point in having a BCP, or BCMS, and any sensible policy must have reasons behind it; those reasons being an integral part of the objectives.

It could be argued that ISO22301 is 'dumbing down' BCM here; almost suggesting that if you haven't got a clear, written set of objectives, you might forget why you are developing a BCM capability, and base your resilience and plans on something else!

That said, where a group of people – and there will usually be a group – develops anything like this, it is generally useful to have a clear set of objectives to maintain focus on the outcome.

The standard also asks for plans to achieve the objectives, which is really what the BCMS is; a plan to achieve the objectives. At this planning stage though, an executive summary is probably what is expected, and again, should prove a useful tool in the development of the system itself.

Support

Having carried out the essential outline planning of what the objectives are, and how they are going to be met, the next stage is to identify the resources, and other capabilities, that will ensure the system does as good a job as possible at delivering the desired results.

Provision of resources

It goes almost without saying that a programme requires resources. ISO22301 requires some evidence that these resources have been determined, and are in place. In addition to the obvious budgetary resources that will be required, roles and responsibilities should be identified, and specific individuals appointed who have the responsibility and authority for:

- 'Ensuring that the management system conforms to the requirements of the international standard, and
- Reporting on the performance of the BCMS to top management.'

It should be borne in mind that these are not necessarily full-time appointments, and will often form a smaller part of one person's responsibilities.

Over and above what the Standard looks for, it will usually make sense, also, to communicate these appointments throughout the organisation. This will help in raising awareness of BCM – a subject to be covered in *Chapter 9*.

Competency of BCM personnel

Clearly, people who are going to be involved in the planning, development, implementation and use of the BCMS, should possess the competencies required to do so.

Very often, however, this is dealt with by an intuitive assessment of an individual's ability to write a procedure, or lead a team. The more systematic and structured approach called for by ISO22301, will ultimately ensure that resource invested in BCM is as effective as possible, and that the resulting BC plans and BCM arrangements are actually fit for purpose.

A simple schedule should be created, setting out the tasks in which individuals might be engaged, and the corresponding competencies that are likely to be required to execute these tasks properly.

An example of a competency schedule can be found in *Appendix 2*.

Awareness and communication

In many organisations, BCM is the preserve of a small number of people who have developed the business continuity plan and resource contingencies, often because there is no formal programme, and because others do not consider that it is anything to do with them.

In the event of a real incident, the outcome is usually that the people who should be using the business continuity plan have little or no knowledge of it, and therefore cannot use it effectively. In addition, the available resources may not be what are actually required, which means that activities cannot be recovered in the way that they should be.

Very few people in the organisation know what they should actually do, so the overall impact of an incident is much greater than it would have been if everyone in the organisation had an appropriate level of understanding and 'ownership' of BCM.

BS25999 referred to this requirement under 'Embedding BCM in the organisation's culture', and ISO22301 addresses the need to get people to treat it as part of their overall working lives, through awareness.

Building genuine awareness is often challenging, and certainly takes some time to achieve. There is, however, often a critical point in awareness raising and engagement at which disinterest turns to interest and active collaboration.

Clearly, a communication programme is an essential part of raising awareness amongst stakeholders, but there should also be communication mechanisms that come into play in the event of an incident. The business continuity procedures that effectively form the BCP, are likely to be most effective if awareness of their communication elements is well understood by anyone affected by them.

Awareness and culture are discussed further in *Chapter 9*.

Documentation

Much of the BCMS, and its requirements, will be in documentary form. Many people find it difficult to locate documents at the best of times, but given the critical nature of many BCM documents, this becomes more acute, and so it makes absolute sense to have a proper, document management system that includes:

- Version control
- Security
- Availability
- Ease of use.

The standard's requirements in this area are more specific, however, the often default route of setting up a set of BCM folders on a network drive, is not likely to produce the desired results.

The document management system will need to include those documents required by the Standard as a minimum.

This subject is discussed further in *Chapter 10*.

Operation

BS25999 launched straight into saying what the core elements of a BCMS should be, without saying that there should be a formal programme, with appropriate operational controls. It did, however, have a more general description of a programme, and referred to it in the BCMS lifecycle, which does not appear in the new standard.

ISO22301 sets out some requirements for operational planning and control which, in simple terms, are that processes (of BCM) should be defined, given criteria, and their completion, or status, documented. The principal procedures are as follows.

Business impact analysis

Any risk control measures, response plans and contingency resources, should ultimately be based upon the relative importance of the activity that they are designed to support. The basis of this element is the business impact analysis (BIA). The BIA should ensure that all activities that the organisation conducts are considered on the same basis, so that none are simply forgotten; and that certain activities are not given unduly high importance, for example, because of the individual responsible.

ISO22301 demands that response plans and contingency arrangements are based upon the outcome of this element, so that the BIA should also establish key details for each activity, including its 'maximum acceptable outage', its resource dependencies and 'single points of failure'.

Many senior managers and executives are tempted to believe that they do not need to conduct an analysis of their organisation. Experience shows, however, that without this element, the resulting plans and arrangements rarely reflect the optimal requirements for recovering the organisation in the event of a major interruption.

Risk assessment

A significant and important part of establishing an organisation's resilience is identifying what can go wrong, and what sort of negative impact these 'going wrong' scenarios might have on the organisation. Distinct from BIA, where we are looking at the impact resulting from interruption of individual business activities, risk assessment is the process of identifying the range of scenarios that could interrupt the organisation's operational activities and what treatment those risks should be given. Treatment may well include BC response capability, but it may also include controls, such as increasing security, moving premises, or training.

BCM strategy

This element is essentially about working out the best way of minimising the impact of interruption on activities, including the provision of key operational resources upon which those activities depend. Although, for the administrative type of organisation, where no real physical processes are involved, this is often relatively straightforward. In other cases, the strategy might be more complex than simply restoring the IT system to a temporary office facility.

ISO22301 states that the strategy should be based on the outputs from the business impact analysis (BIA) and include approval of recovery time-frames. What it doesn't do, is recognise that the strategy for each activity may be different; some activities simply cannot be recovered sufficiently quickly for their outputs also to be resumed, or soon enough to limit impact to an acceptable level. This aspect of strategy can really only be identified when the BIA has been carried out, and this is discussed later in the book.

BCM response

This is, essentially, the business continuity planning element, and, whilst it is a fairly obvious requirement, it is not necessarily a 'no-brainer'. Some organisations prefer to take an entirely fluid approach to response management, on the grounds that every situation is unique, and the number of permutations is almost infinite. Provided such an organisation knows that it has all the required contingencies available, it may satisfy itself that that is good enough.

However, as we shall see, there are several aspects to response management which cannot be left unplanned.

These procedures include a structure and mechanism for response, business continuity plans (BCP), recovery plans and arrangements for exercising, and testing.

A quite significant difference between BS25999 and ISO22301 is that the latter requires procedures to 'return business activities from the temporary measures adopted …', and whilst it doesn't specify returning to the pre-incident operating state, it does refer to supporting normal business requirements.

This may require some strategic thought, as it looks like there is a requirement to move from the 'minimum acceptable level' (of activities) referred to by BS25999, to the pre-incident level, yet many organisations simply would not be able to find reasonable ways of resuming pre-incident activity levels.

Exercising and testing

The importance of this element is also fairly self-evident. Because real incidents or interruptions are uncommon, it makes absolute sense to practise responding from time to time. The element also recognises that organisations change continuously, which means that maintaining plans, contingencies and other arrangements, on a regular basis, is an inevitable requirement. In a real incident situation, one wrong telephone number might lead to a whole sequence of failures, seriously compromising the organisation's response, and its ability to recover.

Performance evaluation and improvement

Consistent with all management systems, ISO22301 requires a methodical approach to continuously monitoring and improving the whole BCMS, relying significantly on documentation to ensure that everything that should happen does. This process is, of course, completely intuitive and makes complete sense, especially in the context of something that isn't somebody's full-time job. But even when it is, good corporate governance dictates that the monitoring of a key risk control system should be visible and fully documented.

Performance evaluation and improvement entails establishing which aspects of the BCMS should be monitored. There are three distinct forms of monitoring:

- Ongoing maintenance – usually of documents and data.
- Internal audit – conducted by people without direct involvement in the development, or operation, of the processes.
- Management review – the more formal review of the entire BCMS, on a regular, planned basis.

These monitoring processes should be supported by a documented improvement system for recording and processing non-conformities and the resulting corrective actions, and a further way of ensuring that the BCMS is continually improved, even when no deficiencies are apparent.

The PDCA cycle

ISO22301, refers additionally to the 'Plan-Do-Check-Act' (PDCA) cycle, which features in a number of British and international management systems standards. PDCA is simply common sense. First, you plan what you are going to do, then you do it, then you check what you have done, and finally you act upon the results of your checking, to improve what you have done.

Essentially, Part 2 requires that each stage of the life cycle is executed using the PDCA model. Whilst this may indeed be how any competent person would approach such a task, the trick is to make sure that there is documented evidence that PDCA has been applied.

Chapter 12, on certification, contains a fuller description of types of evidence and their uses.

Practical programme management

Once an organisation has decided that it will embark upon BCM, a programme of some sort must be established. Because BCM is a 'contingent' discipline, the existence of a proper programme is doubly important.

In organisations where BCM has been sidelined, or delegated, to someone who is not very busy, or who is insufficiently senior, what often happens is that that person is unable to engage the rest of the organisation, so whatever is developed is unlikely to meet the actual needs of the organisation, or to represent good value for money.

An effective programme generally centres around an experienced project or programme manager; usually someone for whom BCM is a substantive, rather than marginal, responsibility, supported by an oversight body with proper authority.

The oversight body might be a committee (or a committee of the Board) specially created for the purpose. It should comprise representatives of all parts of the organisation, for some very sound reasons, including those listed below.

- The actual recovery requirements of each part of the organisation will be properly understood.
- Recovery capabilities provided by support functions will be properly understood.

- Development tasks delegated to different areas are much more likely to be completed.
- The resulting plans will be properly understood by those who would need to use them, and are more likely to reflect actual recovery requirements and priorities.

In addition, the important process of building awareness of BCM, and embedding it in the organisation's culture, is likely to be expedited if each department, division, or section, has a BCM champion amongst them.

Once the programme has been established, the BCM team, however large or small, can then get on with the business of executing the life cycle more effectively, thanks to the support that it can expect from the rest of the organisation.

Set-up phase

A BCM programme can emerge at a wide variety of stages of commitment, development and resourcing. At some point, the organisation's governing body will be persuaded that BCM is a strategic imperative.

In fact, what they are more likely to consider is whether or not the organisation needs to have a BCP, because, to a great many people, the BCP is the primary instrument that ensures that the organisation has the most effective resilience in the face of unforeseen incidents.

Many organisations try to 'get something going' with no additional resource, financial or human, in the hope that a BCP is just a document that should be capable of being put together by someone with a reasonably good knowledge of the organisation. Where this happens, the result is usually a document that, although it is called a business continuity plan, would not be of very much practical use in the event of a real incident.

An increasing number of organisations, however, understand that, for BCM to be effective, it requires a properly established and resourced programme that is treated as part of the organisation, rather than some 'special project' that has little to do with the core business.

The programme manager should establish an appropriate oversight body, as early as possible. This might well be a committee, ideally a subcommittee of the Board, with authority to act upon its decisions, and including representatives from all parts of the organisation.

One of the committee's first tasks should be to formulate policy, unless this has already been completed by the Board. In any case, this policy should, ideally, be approved formally by the Board. Policy is described in more detail later on.

The 'rump' of the programme in the early stages is effectively the first iteration of the life cycle.

Although, in smaller organisations, subsequent iterations may amount to minor adjustments only, these may elsewhere be more substantive, as the scope of BCM is broadened progressively, in order to develop and prove the concept of BCM before roll-out to the entire organisation.

The key tasks for the programme manager and the oversight body or committee, are the seven principal sections of the Standard:

- Context of the organisation
- Leadership
- Planning

- Support
- Operation
- Performance evaluation
- Improvement.

In many cases, it will make sense to complete work associated with the first four of these sections, before embarking on the subsequent development and operation of BCM processes and their improvement mechanisms.

Typically, these first four sections might be approached more as a project, with a defined start, middle and end; and the subsequent three as an ongoing programme. In reality, the first four sections should be revisited on a regular basis, as part of the management review process at least.

Ongoing/maintenance phase

Even with a well-established BCM programme, there is a tendency for it to lose momentum and to be sidelined after the initial launch of the BCP. People who may have been enthusiastic participants in its development, which is often the only part in which they are interested, will return to their normal routine feeling pleased that the BCP, BCM or DR 'box' has been ticked.

Maintenance of a BCM programme is much akin to maintenance of anything else. It takes a relatively small amount of effort, on a regular basis, to keep it fit for purpose, but, if left, it becomes increasingly unfit for purpose, and requires a significant amount of effort and resource to get back to serviceability. This is not only common sense, it is also a key part of the return on investment in adopting a good practice approach to BCM.

End products

In the earlier days of business continuity, the BCP was all that really mattered. In reality, most organisations that had a BCP had a document with *Business Continuity Plan* on the front cover. Inside, the document would often express intentions about returning to business as usual, as quickly as possible, but these so-called 'plans' would not be particularly useful in the event of a real incident.

In today's business and public sector environments, the culture of good governance, accountability, and corporate and social responsibility, means that the old way simply is not good enough.

The BCP remains a key deliverable, not least because, without one, the organisation cannot respond properly to an unforeseen incident. However, another key deliverable today is assurance. The governing body, shareholders, customers and all other stakeholders, now want some assurance that, as well as the organisation's financial viability being properly managed, the significant operational risks of business interruption are also being managed in the most appropriate way. This assurance is most powerfully supported by some independent verification that the BCP exists, is fit for purpose, and has been developed according to good practice. Certification under ISO22301 is undoubtedly the ultimate form of assurance, but any assurance mechanism is now a key deliverable from the programme.

Resources

This book attempts to dispel a number of myths, probably the greatest of which is that BCM can be 'done' with effectively no additional resource.

Many organisations have attempted a BCM programme using purely existing resources, with the fairly common and inevitable result that very little of value is achieved, and that it does, in fact, cost money. Like any new discipline that becomes an inevitable feature of business or public service, BCM has to be seen as an essential part of risk management, and of economic growth. The level of resource required for BCM depends, naturally, upon the size, nature and complexity of the organisation.

- Large organisations often make best use of resources by employing one or more full-time, BCM professionals.
- Medium-sized organisations may include BCM as a key responsibility for an operational manager or director, with a degree of outsourced expertise and programme development.
- Smaller organisations may outsource the entire development process, engaging staff and key managers through the oversight body (committee), and throughout the execution of each stage in the life cycle.

The best approach, where possible, is to establish a budget for BCM, either as part of general risk management, or as a stand-alone item. It should also be remembered that savings delivered through the application of good practice, should also be associated to that budget, so that its true cost and value can be properly assessed.

In addition to this programme resourcing, the engagement of staff throughout the organisation should also be treated as a resource requirement. The fact is that some key staff will need to spend time executing tasks that contribute to the BCM programme; it is arguably better that this resource requirement is visible, than for the programme to struggle because these already busy people simply do not have the time to complete BCM-related activities as well.

Governance and assurance processes

Despite the apparent weight of corporate governance as a driver in developing a BCM programme, the Standard actually makes little mention of it, suggesting that it is about assigning responsibility.

In reality, directors and governors are expected to know that risks are being managed, with some idea of how. In most cases, directors and governors hope, or perhaps assume, that all risks are being managed appropriately.

A sensible addition to the role of the oversight body or committee, is that it should report to the governing body, on a regular basis, the state of the BCM programme, and therefore the extent to which, *inter alia*, the business interruption risks are being managed.

Successful certification under ISO22301 does provide a very high level of assurance in this respect, albeit as a 'snapshot'. Equally important is the ongoing and regular assurance that, through proper maintenance and testing of the BCM arrangements and the management review process, these risks continue to be properly managed.

A potential pitfall in the application of documented standards is their 'normative' reference to other documents, so that reference to these normative documents is mandatory for successful certification. As in the case of

BS25999, ISO22301 has no such references, and can therefore be implemented more or less in isolation, unless an integrated management systems approach is being adopted, in which case reference to the other, relevant, management system standards, is clearly necessary.

CHAPTER 3: BUSINESS IMPACT ANALYSIS AND RISK ASSESSMENT

These elements are really pivotal in a good BCMS. Without them, there can be no assurance that all potential interruption scenarios have been taken into account, nor that the resilience, response and recovery capabilities are comprehensive, and based on the true priorities of the organisation.

Business impact analysis

The simple premise of business impact analysis (BIA) is that the BCM arrangements for each activity should be commensurate with the impact of interrupting that activity. This section looks at what BIA is for, and how to conduct it.

What is BIA?

As its name suggests, BIA involves the analysis of the impacts sustained when activities are interrupted. Of course, there are many other types of impact and situations when they may be sustained, but, in the context of BCM, this is what BIA is.

In order to analyse these impacts, it is necessary to understand what we are looking for. When an activity is interrupted, there is likely to be a negative impact, perhaps not immediately, but after a certain period of time. In commercial organisations, that impact might conveniently be expressed in financial terms, but, elsewhere, other ways of measuring impact may also be required.

It is also usually the case that the longer the interruption continues, the greater the impact, so that each activity has a time-based impact profile. At a very basic level, it is then possible to see, and understand, the impact that would be sustained if some, or all, of an organisation's activities were interrupted, regardless of the cause.

Figure 3 illustrates a simple, impact timeline, showing the equivalent financial impact for each of five different activities, should they be interrupted, at selected points along the timeline, starting from the Business as Usual (BaU) level of zero.

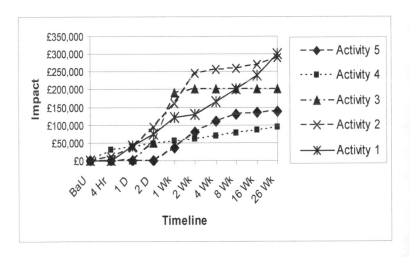

Figure 3: Impact profile 1

This sort of data can be very useful in revealing the relative importance, or criticality, of individual activities. It can also then be used to look at the cumulative impacts, for example, if the entire organisation were to be interrupted.

However, in many organisations, the interdependence and complexity of activities is such that analysis of these activities individually, is rather difficult to do, and very often the total impact is not the same as the sum of the parts, as you can see in *Figure 4*.

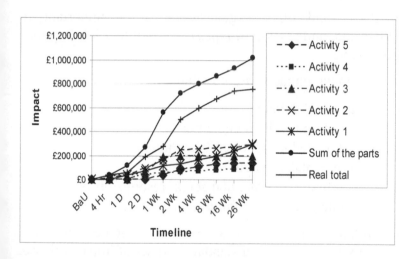

Figure 4: Impact profile 2

Whilst the BIA can be useful in calculating the maximum impact, or loss, in the event of complete organisational interruption, its real purpose, in BCM terms, is to establish the relative priority for recovering different activities or business processes.

Non-financial impacts

Impacts that are not immediately identifiable as financial in nature, may carry more weight in some organisations than in others. Of course, for the majority of commercially-driven organisations, these impacts eventually have some financial impact, perhaps as customers gradually turn to other suppliers, or market confidence leads to a reduction in the share price.

In these, and other organisations, it is important to understand, and assess, all types of impact that interruptions might have.

Non-financial impacts might include:

- Reputational damage
- Reduction in levels of customer service
- Loss of accreditation or certification
- Environmental damage
- Reduction in corporate and social responsibility
- Corporate governance failure.

The relative weight of these impacts must be considered carefully in drawing up a standardised set of impact criteria. These criteria are essential in ensuring that assessments of the impact resulting from a range of interruption scenarios are objective, and not unduly skewed by any individual's ideas about how critical particular activities may be.

The starting point is to establish a scale of impact levels; the most common approach in the context of BCM is a five-point scale. Against this scale, a broad definition for each level is needed, so that assessors can judge, as accurately as possible, how severe a particular impact is. The table in *Figure 5* shows how this might result.

It is for each organisation to decide whether impact definitions, such as those in Figure 5, are suitable for it, though they are likely to be fairly close to the mark for the majority.

Level	Name	Definition
5	Catastrophic	Loss of business value that is liable to terminate the organisation's existence
4	Intolerable	Loss of business value exceeding the organisation's tolerance, but from which it is likely, eventually, to recover
3	Major	Major loss of business value
2	Significant	Significant loss of business value
1	Minor	Minor loss of business value

Figure 5: Scale of impact levels

In practical terms, though, it may be more useful to translate these impact levels into more specific indicators, not least so that individuals with a narrower perspective on the organisation, can select levels, in terms that they more readily understand.

The table in *Figure 6* shows an impact criteria table, with three different types of impact. This kind of table enables anyone conducting an impact assessment to assign an impact scale of between 1 and 5, in a number of different ways.

Level	Name	Financial (£)	Reputation	Service standards (% below target)
5	Catastrophic	Over 500,000	National media coverage; product withdrawal	>20
4	Intolerable	200,001 to 500,000	Vertical or sustained local media coverage; complaints to relevant authorities	15.5-20
3	Major	75,001 to 200,000	Local media coverage; increase in customer complaints >100%	13.5-15
2	Significant	25,001 to 75,000	Increase in customer complaints <100%	10.5-13
1	Minor	Under 25,000	Increase in customer complaints <50%	<10

Figure 6: Impact criteria table

Figure 7 shows that applying these criteria to the example in *Figure 3*, would give a similar, though more granular picture, of the organisation's time-based impact profile. The small version of the original is included for reference.

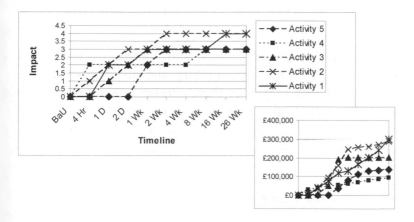

Figure 7: Impact profile 3

Impact treatment

In a case where there are a number of different impact types, the way in which impacts are treated should be standardised, so that it can be built into the data collection methodology.

The options for assessment include:

- Deciding whether a given activity is most sensitive to a particular impact type, and collecting only that data.
- Recording the highest impact from one of the types, at each point on the timeline.
- Recording impacts in all types, then choosing the highest during analysis.

- Recording impacts in all types, and then calculating a simple, or weighted average, during analysis.

It may be tempting to try to collect impacts of every type, at every point on the timeline, for every activity, but this needs to be balanced against the need to get the job done; to minimise the additional workload for otherwise busy people.

A simple and reasonably successful approach is to present the assessor with a table, showing the meaning of all the impacts, so that they can then choose one level at each timeline point. If the impact criteria table has been well constructed, it should not matter whether the chosen impact level is financial, for example, or reputational in scale.

Identifying the activities

This is perhaps the most challenging aspect of conducting a BIA. Having established some standardised criteria for assessing the impact resulting from interruptions to activities, surely one could simply give these to the people responsible for managing those activities, and let them make the best assessment? This may work in some organisations, but, more often, it immediately raises questions about what is actually being assessed. What are the activities, or processes, that are to be assessed in this way?

Many practitioners in BCM, and the Standard itself, suggest that organisations execute some activities which are critical, and others which are not. This binary approach to identifying activities is questionable, particularly when one considers the Standard's definition of critical activities as:

... those activities which have to be performed in order to deliver the key products and services which enable an organisation to meet its most important, and time-sensitive, objectives.

The majority of organisations feature activities with varying levels of importance or criticality, and 'critical' is not an absolute term – some things are more critical than others.

So the question arises: Does one decide, first, which activities are critical, then assess the impacts arising from their interruption; or does one assess the impacts arising from the interruption of all, or most, of the organisation's activities, thus establishing a scale of criticality of all processes?

A potential danger of the former approach is that certain activities which, if assessed, would turn out to be quite critical, are missed, because, in the absence of any analysis, they are deemed to be non-critical.

The starting point is therefore usually the scope, referred to in *Chapter 2*, which may have narrowed the focus of the BCM activity down to various operational parts of the organisation that are covered by the BCM programme, and therefore the BIA. However, there then has to be some classification of activities, or business processes, that can be assessed for impact.

This is individual to every organisation, and can be a major piece of work in itself. At this point, the temptation often arises to simply decide what the recovery priorities and requirements are for the various organisational functions, but it must be remembered that the Standard calls for the results of the BIA to inform the planning process.

There can be no standard way of identifying activities, but it makes sense to keep things as simple as possible. Some organisations operate a number of almost independent teams, departments or functions, that can be easily identified and analysed separately, but, in many others, these entities are interdependent, and all contribute to the same eventual products and services that the organisation exists to deliver.

If there is a rule of thumb, it is probably that one should start at the top of the organisation, and look at the main divisions or departments, to see whether each could be assessed for impacts as an entity, or whether it comprises many different activities that should be assessed individually. Working down through the organisation's structure, it should be possible to find the highest, common denominator, which may well be at different levels between, and within, main divisions or departments.

Where physical processes are involved, the primary difference will usually be that they depend upon different resources from administrative-type activities. In a manufacturing business, for example, one might assess a complete production line, rather than one individual machine within the line.

This approach, based on the jobs that people or, in some cases, machines do, should result in the minimum number of assessments being required. It should also ensure that all the organisation's activities are considered. *Figure 8* illustrates one way of establishing an organisation's activities, which can then be assessed for interruption impacts.

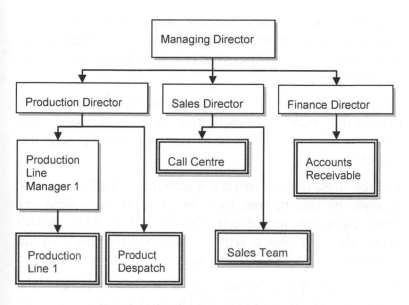

Figure 8: Organisational activities

In this rather simplified example, activities are indicated by a double-lined box. Defining activities in this context is both intuitive and reiterative. It is quite likely that, once an activity has been defined, analysis of the impact of it being interrupted, reveals that it would be much easier to assess it as two separate activities.

The importance of this becomes clearer when one considers the resource requirements for individual activities. Following an interruption, a team of people who execute a number of activities, might need to be operational within a short timescale, because of the criticality of one of their activities. The other resources required for this one activity, such as IT applications, telecommunications, information sources, and so on, would also be required in that short timescale. However, the resources required for other activities that the team performed, might not be required so quickly, because these other activities were not as critical. Higher or quicker availability of resources often means more cost, and cost-effectiveness is usually an objective in any BCM programme.

So, there is a balance to be struck between identifying a manageable number of activities on the one hand, and achieving cost-effectiveness of resource contingencies on the other.

The job of setting out what the activities actually are, may be done by one person, by a BCM team, or, indeed, by those responsible for the activities themselves. This, as with many other disciplines, will depend upon the nature of the organisation and how it is managed.

From the BCM practitioner's point of view, it is desirable that managers of activities decide, and set out, what the activities are, though in many cases, they will need some rules and guidance from the BCM practitioner or co-ordinator.

Suppliers

Many organisations outsource some of their activities to suppliers or providers, often including activities that support products and services. These suppliers' services should also be treated as activities within the BIA, since their interruption will have the same impact on the organisation, whether executed by the organisation, or by a third party.

Where this is the case, it will be important to establish a suitable, supplier assurance activity in respect of BCM (*see Chapter 9*).

Collecting the data

At the most basic level, this can be done by way of a spreadsheet, with a simple table into which impact levels may be entered, as in *Figure 9*.

Activity Classification		Timeline								
Division	Activity	4 Hr	1 D	2 D	1 Wk	2 Wk	4 Wk	8 Wk	16 Wk	26 Wk
Finance	Accounts receivable	1	1	2	4	5	5	5	5	5
Production	Product despatch	1								
Finance	Cash management	0								
Production	Production line 1	1								
Finance	Payroll	0								
Production	Production line 2	1								
Production	Production line 3	1								
Sales	Call centre - inward	1								
Sales	Order processing	0								
Finance	Credit control	0								
Sales	Call centre - outward	0								
Finance	Accounts payable	0								
Finance	Management accounts	0								
Sales	Brochure pack fulfilment	0								
Sales	Sample fulfilment	0								

Level	Financial (£)	Reputational	Service (% below target)
5	Over 500,000	National media coverage Product withdrawal	Over 20
4	200,001 - 500,00	Vertical or sustained local media coverage Complaints to relevant authorities	15.5 – 20
3	75,001 - 200,000	Local media coverage Increase in customer complaints >100%	13.5 – 15
2	25,001 - 75,000	Increase in customer complaints up to 100%	10.5 – 13
1	Up to 25,000	Increase in customer complaints up to 50%	Up to 10

Figure 9: Simple BIA spreadsheet

In reality, of course, there would be considerably more activities to be assessed than this, but the example shows how impact assessments can be captured simply, and, most importantly, based on standardised criteria, so they are as objective as possible.

This collected data can then be analysed, and used to inform the strategy and response planning processes, by determining the time-frame for recovery of the activity(ies) in question, or of their outputs, dependent upon the strategy. BS25999 referred to this time-frame as the 'maximum tolerable period of disruption' (MTPD), and whilst this term is included in ISO22301's list of terms, it isn't used in the Standard itself. Nonetheless, it remains a perfectly valid term to describe, in the context of the new standard, the time-frame within which activities must be recovered, in order to prevent intolerably, high impacts accruing.

Impact data analysis

Figure 10 shows a graphical representation of the data from *Figure 9*.

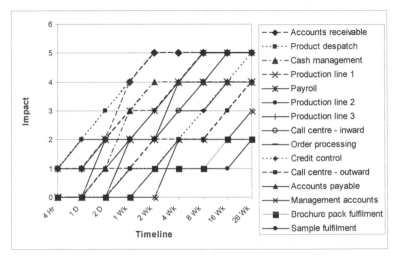

Figure 10: Impact profile 4

What can now be analysed is the impact profile, that is to say, the rate at which the impact for each activity increases over time.

If we were to set an impact threshold and apply it to all the activities in *Figure 10*, by drawing a horizontal line across the chart at the impact threshold level of 2, we would then be able to see what the MTPD was in each case. The results are shown in *Figure 11*.

Activity Classification			Timeline					
Division	Activity	MTPD	4 Hr	1 D	2 D	1 Wk	2 Wk	4 Wk
Finance	Accounts receivable	2 D	1	1	2	4	5	
Production	Product despatch	2 D	1	2	3	4	5	5
Finance	Cash management	1 Wk	0	0	1	3	4	4
Production	Production line 1	1 Wk	1	1	2	3	3	4
Finance	Payroll	2 Wk	0	0	2	2	2	4
Production	Production line 2	2 Wk	1	1	1	2	3	4
Production	Production line 3	2 Wk	1	2	2	2	3	4
Sales	Call centre - inward	4 Wk	1	1	2	2	2	3
Sales	Order processing	4 Wk	0	0	0	2	2	3
Finance	Credit control	8 Wk	0	0	0	1	1	
Sales	Call centre - outward	16 Wk	0	0	1	1	2	2
Finance	Accounts payable	26 Wk	0	0	0	0	1	2
Finance	Management accounts	26 Wk	0	0	0	0	0	
Sales	Brochure pack fulfilment	26 Wk	0	0	0	0	1	1
Sales	Sample fulfilment	26 Wk	0	0	0	1	1	1

Figure 11: Impact threshold applied

Now, by sorting this data in ascending order of MTPD, we can create a recovery timeline which can then directly inform the planning process, as shown in *Figure 12*.

This is precisely how the results of a BIA can be used to inform the strategy selection and planning processes, though it should be remembered that, in this example, the setting of the impact tolerance threshold at 2 is somewhat arbitrary.

If a threshold of 3 were to be tried instead, this would give the results shown in *Figure 13*.

What can be seen, is that the priority order is different between the two, which is because of the way that the impacts for each activity change over time.

The resulting timeline can now form the basis for a BCP. First, however, the availability of the resources required to support these activities must be established.

Activity	MTPD
Accounts receivable	2 D
Product despatch	2 D
Cash management	1 Wk
Production line 1	1 Wk
Payroll	2 Wk
Production line 2	2 Wk
Production line 3	2 Wk
Call centre – inward	4 Wk
Order processing	4 Wk
Credit control	8 Wk
Call centre – outward	16 Wk
Accounts payable	26 Wk
Management accounts	26 Wk
Brochure pack fulfilment	26 Wk
Sample fulfilment	26 Wk

Timeline

Figure 12: Recovery timeline 1

Activity	MTPD
Production line 3	1 D
Product despatch	1 D
Payroll	2 D
Accounts receivable	2 D
Cash management	2 D
Production line 1	2 D
Call centre – inward	2 D
Production line 2	1 Wk
Call centre – outward	2 Wk
Credit control	4 Wk
Accounts payable	4 Wk
Management accounts	4 Wk
Order processing	4 Wk
Brochure pack fulfilment	16 Wk
Sample fulfilment	26 Wk

Figure 13: Recovery timeline 2

Recovery time objectives

The maximum tolerable period of disruption is based upon the impact resulting from interruption reaching a threshold, or maximum tolerable level. It may make sense, in many cases, to set an objective for partial, or complete, recovery of the activity in question that is within this MTPD timescale. For example, if a team of people are redeployed to a temporary location equipped with the resources that they need, it may take some time for them to reconcile information and make other preparations, before they are able to execute the relevant activity in more or less the usual way. Many organisations feel they would simply prefer to build some time contingency into their recovery plans, and, for these reasons, the recovery time objective (RTO) may be shorter than the MTPD.

Ultimately, ISO22301 stipulates a requirement for a 'prioritised time-frame', and the use of any suitable term, including RTO, should cause no concern.

Partial and full recovery

Whilst most organisations would prefer to recover their activities fully, as soon as possible after an interruptive incident, the extent to which this is achievable will depend upon many factors, and, in some cases, is simply not feasible. However, in order that DR and other contingency resources can be established, a statement of the minimum activity- or service-level, is an important consideration, otherwise the resources will drive the activity rather than vice versa.

This minimum, activity level is often unwritten, but, in order that the adequacy and effectiveness of the BCM arrangements can be verified, it should be stated wherever possible.

A statement of normal activity levels is also helpful, so that plans can provide clear information about the extent to which further recovery is required.

The standard does require plans to return from the temporary arrangements used in response, though it stops short of saying 'to the original operational state', referring instead to 'support normal business requirements'. In the context of BIA, this reinforces the need to document normal levels of activity as the starting point, or baseline.

Tools

Depending upon the complexity of the organisation, it may be appropriate to invest in an appropriate IT tool with which to conduct BIA.

Here, caution is advised. At the time of writing, there are few tools available that have been developed specifically for this purpose, and which actually deliver the required results. There are numerous offerings available, and it is quite likely that one could find a spreadsheet template for sale that purports to be a comprehensive, BIA tool.

An appropriate tool should include, at least, the following functionality:

- Standard impact assessment criteria, and the ability to assess activities against them, without having to remember the definition of each level.
- Activity- or business-process records, in a variety of categories and subcategories.
- Ability to show interdependency between activities.

- Calculation and/or presentation of time-based impact profiles.
- 'What if?' impact tolerance modelling, presenting MTPD/RTO profiles based on different thresholds.

Other areas of functionality, applying to the resource planning element of 'understanding the organisation and its context', are discussed in *Chapter 2*. If a tool does not offer at least some capability to analyse the impacts, then one should ask whether it is worth the price, or indeed the investment in time to learn how to use it.

The role of insurance

In assessing the impact attributable to interrupting activities, it may be appropriate to consider the mitigating effect of business interruption insurance. Where there is a straightforward loss of gross profit resulting from an incident, this type of insurance cover would generally reduce that loss, which could lead to the MTPD being increased. Extreme caution is advised in this area, as insurance policy conditions may vary widely, and an organisation that does nothing to limit its losses in the event of an incident, may well find it difficult to achieve settlement of its claim.

More important than this, though, is the fact that virtually all business interruption insurance policies provide no indemnity against the loss of future business, resulting directly, or indirectly, from an interruptive incident.

Many policies may also exclude a variety of reasons for loss, such as failure of an IT system. In some cases, the failure of an IT system may bring the organisation to a halt operationally, thus losing gross profit in the process, and yet the business interruption insurance policy may not cover this type of interruption.

In the most severe cases, some loss of profit is inevitable, so insurance certainly has its place, but organisations should consider the relative value of BCM, as potentially a more cost-effective way of mitigating the losses more generally attributable to interruptive incidents.

Disaster recovery resources

It goes virtually without saying that organisations require resources to enable their activities to be conducted. For many, these would comprise:

- People
- Information
- Information processing tools
- A working environment.

For others, they might include:

- Handling and processing facilities
- Plant and equipment
- Distribution capability.

Many people have experienced a short-term loss of one or more of these resources, and so are familiar with the disabling effect it can have on conducting business as usual. All the same, there are many ill-conceived business continuity plans in existence that seem to take little account of the need to have these resources in place.

We should also distinguish between normal levels of activity, utility and comfort, and an interim recovery environment designed to enable a minimum, or perhaps reduced, level of activity to continue.

A sensible starting point is often to record, or map, the resources that are available to, and used by, each defined activity. This can be an endless exercise, particularly when one considers, not just the primary resources, such as computers, desks, telephones, information, vehicles and so on, but also the wide variety of lesser items, such as stationery, books and hand tools.

Decisions need to be taken on the categorisation of resources, so that those responsible for managing activities can clearly identify what they would need in the event of a disruption.

Again, this is specific to the organisation, but there are a number of fairly obvious categories that apply to the vast majority, including:

- Workspace
- 'Seats' (desk, chair, etc.)
- Meeting and presentation facilities
- Utilities and other services
- Computers or terminals
- IT applications and data
- Hard copy information, including unique documents
- Printers and other peripherals
- Stationery
- People
- Telephones
- Voice and data telecommunications capability
- Money and cash
- Vehicles
- Machines, plant and equipment

- Raw materials
- Consumables used in processing, packaging and distribution.

The simple logic here is that the resources, whether the original ones or replacements, need to be available for use when the activity in question requires them. Availability usually costs money, and there is a relationship between the level of availability (how much, how soon) and cost. This means that the identification of when replacement resources are actually required, is an important process.

As intimated previously, a very common mistake with BC planning is to set out what resources would be required in the event of a significant disruption, without putting in place arrangements that will ensure, as far as possible, that the required resources will actually be available, together with the procedures or instructions for invoking those resources.

Mapping and analysis

Depending upon the size, nature and complexity of the organisation, this can be a relatively straightforward process.

Mapping means assigning resources to activities that use them and, whilst BaU resource levels may be pertinent, it is the resources required to deliver the minimum acceptable level of activity that are most important. Figure 14 shows how basic resource information can be collected using a spreadsheet, together with a simple, data validation function that allows users to select only valid names for resources.

Activity	Office			Applications		
	No Seat	PCs	Phone	1	2	3
Accounts receivable	6	6	4	email	File server	Internet
Product despatch	8	2	2	Database	MRP	
Cash management	2	2	2	email	File server ▼	ernet
Production line 1	16	1	2	MRP	email	
Payroll	2	2	2	Payroll	File server Internet	
Production line 2	20	1	2	MRP	Database	
Production line 3	9	0	1	MRP	Hr system Payroll	
Call centre - inward	15	15	15	email	MRP	e server
Order processing	4	4	2	Database	MRP	email
Credit control	2	2	2	email	Database	Internet
Call centre - outward	26	26	26	email	Database	
Accounts payable	3	3	2	email	Database	Internet
Management accounts	2	2	2	Database	MRP	File server
Brochure pack fulfilment	4	1	1	Database		
Sample fulfilment	2	1	1	Database		

Figure 14: Basic resource mapping spreadsheet

Of course, desks, telephones, computers and most peripherals, are relatively generic items which can usually be obtained on a contingency basis from a suitable DR provider. The sort of resources that are used in processing, and the like, are not usually so readily available. In formulating the recovery strategy (*see Chapter 4*), it is generally important to capture relevant information about resources that would normally support these activities.

This information should be useful in establishing the availability of alternative resources, even down to the level of spare parts that might be required to get a processing or manufacturing facility running again after a failure.

Ultimately, the providers of resources, whether internal departments (such as IT, facilities management and engineering), or third-party providers, will need to be in possession of a list of recovery resource requirements, including timescales, with which to cost and then arrange their availability. Again, this may well be a reiterative process, as the cost of providing the resource availability required is identified as being too high, or outside the budget. In that event, one would ideally go back to the analysis of impact data and raise the impact threshold, so that MTPDs increase and, with them, the availability requirements for some, or all, resources. This approach effectively applies budgetary limitations evenly across the resource availability spectrum, and is likely to have the most even effect on activity recovery times. The principle behind this is that it is better to marginally increase the recovery timescale for all activities than to significantly increase it for one, or a small number, of activities.

More sophisticated modelling might be able to produce the optimal resource availability combination, but it is unlikely that sufficient data on the different levels and costs of resource availability would be available for this purpose.

Ultimately, this is an area where judgement and intuition, combined with the application of the principles, is likely to result in the most pragmatic solution.

Identifying resources

This is another area where judgement is required; at one extreme, one could list every single computer, monitor, keyboard, printer, and so on, as well as furniture, and all sorts of other resources supporting the activity. On the other hand, one could be too brief, referring, for example, to 'the accounts office' as a resource.

As ever, balance is required, and, for office or administrative resources, things are relatively straightforward. Referring to a 'seat', which means a desk and chair, possibly with a telephone and PC or terminal, will work for many organisations. If, however, different users have different specifications of PC, then it may be necessary to refer to 'high' or 'standard' spec PCs.

Keeping it generic usually makes the mapping and planning process simpler, but, ultimately, both the provider(s) of those resources, BaU and contingency, and the users, will need to understand exactly what is meant by a 'high spec PC' or a '35 CFM air compressor'.

A sensible starting point is the people or departments that provide the resources, typically IT, facilities, engineering, human resources, and so on. These people are usually well placed to set out the semi-generic descriptions of the resources that the organisation uses from day to day. Owners, or managers, of the activities can then state, or confirm, which items they actually depend upon, and with which ones they could deliver the minimum, acceptable level of activity.

Many resources, though, may have a 'tolerance' associated with them. That is to say that the activity in question would need the given resource, but that the activity could be recovered, or resumed, a specified amount of time before that resource is available. This may be important from a cost-effectiveness point of view, since, as we have already seen, availability usually costs money, and savings could be made if a resource that is not required immediately upon resumption of the activity, is made available later, reducing the cost of availability.

Conflicts

There are some fairly common traps to fall into when it comes to DR or resource contingency planning. Particularly in larger organisations, planning may be conducted in 'silos', so that one department or division assumes that a resource that is known to exist would be available to it as a contingency. However, at the same time, another department may make the same assumption. These assumptions may be accidentally safe, but, unless all the assumptions used in BC planning are tested, the plans themselves cannot truly be considered robust.

This is an area where computer-based tools, discussed in the next section, can make a very valuable contribution, particularly if they are collaborative in nature.

Tools

We have already looked briefly at tools in the context of analysing impacts, but it generally makes sense that any tool should also be capable of analysing the resource requirements to respond to the contingency.

Ideally, the tool would be capable of presenting a comprehensive schedule of contingency resource requirements, showing conflicts and gaps, and should also have the ability to model variations in availability levels against costs. It should be able to do this for the entire organisation, as well as at division, department or other structural level, and to consider the relative robustness of resources shared between physically separate sites.

Again, at the time of writing, there is no known tool available that provides this level of functionality. All the same, at the opposite end of the spectrum from simple templates purporting to be suitable tools, no doubt some providers of enterprise-level software would at least claim to be able to provide this sort of functionality within their products. IT Governance Ltd (*www.itgovernance.co.uk*) says that it is developing just such a tool, but it was not available for review, or testing, at the time of finalising this book.

Risk identification, assessment and management

What is risk?

There are many books, articles, papers and opinions, written about risk. In every, single thing that all of us do, all the time, there is a risk that things will go worse than we had hoped or expected.

A risk comprises two things: the likelihood that an unexpected, or undesirable, event will occur, and the negative impact likely to be experienced if it does.

The widely accepted definition of risk is:

Risk (score) = Likelihood (%) x Impact

To illustrate this, let us look at a well-known example of Chance (*see Example 2*).

Example 2 illustrates the practical value of quantifying a risk, rather than assessing it intuitively – the results are often different. Please see the *Introduction* for an interpretation of the patterns used in place of colours in the printed version of this book.

Example 2: Risk, likelihood and impact

A bet of £2.00 on horse A, at odds of 5:1, would result in winnings of £10.00. Odds of 5:1 (against winning) mean that the likelihood of the horse winning the race is 20%.

Similarly, a bet of £4.00 on horse B, at odds of 5:2, would also result in winnings of £10.00. Because this horse is 40% likely to win the race, many of us would be prepared to risk more money for the same winnings.

But looking at the negative aspect of this risk, the likelihood of losing on horse A is 80% and the impact would be £2, and the likelihood of losing on horse B is 60% and the impact would be £4.

These risks are represented in Matrix A, below:

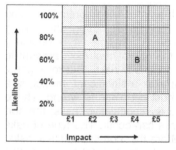

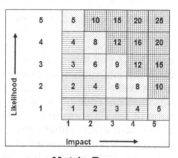

Matrix A   **Matrix B**

However, if we look at the accepted definition of risk, where risk = likelihood x impact; risk A is £1.60 and risk B is £2.40. It is worse, or higher, than risk A. This corresponds with a typical, risk scoring matrix (Matrix B) where, on impact and likelihood scales of 1 to 5, the highest risk score is 25 and the lowest is 1. In these terms, risk A would be scored at 8 and risk B at 12.

Risk appetite (willingness to take a risk) depends, to some extent, upon whether we have to perform the risky activity ourselves. In the example of betting on a horse, most of us do not gamble for a living, so it does not matter if we do not do it. But in the organisational context, be it a commercial business or, perhaps, a public sector organisation, it does matter if we do not do what we are there to do.

This is where we should start to look at the different types of risks that organisations face.

Example 3 concerns a property developer who buys houses, improves them, and then sells them.

Example 3: Operational and strategic risks

The developer faces core business risks: that a given house does not increase in value as expected, and, when sold, does not generate the required profit, or even makes a loss.

It also faces operational risks, such as a building contractor going out of business, or a material supplier ordering the wrong materials, extending the project completion time. It is relatively easy to see, in this example, that the operational risks amount to business interruption or business continuity risks. But to suggest that a bad purchase, which also makes a significant impact, is a business continuity risk, would almost certainly be wrong. These sorts of risks are usually described as 'speculative' risks; the sort of risk from which either profit or loss can occur. The type of risks that are the proper subject of BCM are the 'non-speculative' risks, the risks from which only loss or harm can follow. It is this approach that is reflected in the spirit of the Standard.

Practical operational risk management

As we have seen, the positive aspect of speculative risk really amounts to doing what the organisation is there to do. From a BCM perspective, we need only consider the negative aspects of these risks, the non-speculative risks, which is why we are looking at the likelihood of an unwanted event and negative impact, if it occurs.

All organisational activities carry a variety of risks – arguably more so in the case of commercial organisations. Risk management though, is not particularly scientific. It is simply the case that **activities** may have **vulnerabilities** that may be exploited by **threats**, which, should they materialise, will give rise to some negative **impact**. These really are the key words of risk assessment, and the Standard also refers to the risk assessment approach set out in ISO/IEC 27001:2005

We have already looked at a numerical technique for scoring risks; however, in order to conduct risk management at the organisational level, a structured approach is required.

Risk identification

In the context of BCM, the first step is to identify the risks of business interruption, which the policy will define. We will see later the importance of the objective assessment of risk, and this is also facilitated by the development of a **risk register**, which will be discussed later in this chapter.

The risk register is a sensible repository for business interruption risk information, our area of interest here, though it can also be used for any type of risk.

Depending upon the nature, size and complexity of the organisation, the risk register may be a simple list of risks that have been identified, and which can subsequently have attributed to them an objective assessment of the severity of that risk.

Essentially, one or more individuals have got to consider the organisation, and identify things that could go wrong, that fall within the scope of BCM and would lead to an interruption of the organisation's activities. These risks may conveniently be categorised in a number of ways, including:

- Major incidents – fire, explosion, flood, structural collapse, terrorist acts, including chemical, biological, radiological and nuclear (CBRN) contamination.
- Resource failures – utilities, information systems, telecommunications, supply chain, processing facilities.
- Environmental – extremes of weather, gas leaks, other contamination, infestation.
- Denial of access – security incidents, legal disputes, access closures, accident or crime investigations.
- Civil emergencies – pandemic influenza or other disease, civil unrest.
- Product compromise – deliberate or accidental contamination, extortion.

There are likely to be more risks of business interruption, depending upon the nature of the organisation, its customers, suppliers, location, markets, and so on.

Risk identification should be as comprehensive as possible; ideally every risk that the organisation faces should be identified. However, there is no guaranteed way of identifying every risk, not least because there are usually so many. Those involved in identifying risks have to come up with things that could go wrong, and that would then make a significant impact on the organisation – at least to the lowest level on the standardised impact scale.

Techniques for identifying risks include the following:

- Questionnaires
- Brainstorming workshops
- Building and site inspections

- Input from other management systems, such as quality, environmental and security
- 'Whistle-blowing' policies
- Use of third-party assessors.

There can be no guarantee that every single risk that an organisation faces has been identified, but the spirit in which this should be approached, is one of 'best endeavours' and reasonableness. So, if you make a proper effort to identify every risk, and simply miss something because no one thought of it, then, from a corporate governance or audit point of view, that is probably acceptable; nobody should be accused of negligence.

Scope

BCM is widely understood to be a discipline that protects the organisation against the impacts of unforeseen incidents and events of an operational or, perhaps, physical nature. The Standard emphatically focuses on products and services, which means that the BCMS should deal with the organisation's ability to continue delivering its products and/or services.

The inference from this, is that risks posed by threats that, although they might adversely affect the organisation, would not compromise its ability to continue delivering products and/or services, should not be included in the scope of risk assessment, or of BCM generally.

However, it must ultimately be for the organisation to decide if certain risks, whether operational, financial, strategic or anything else in nature, should be controlled to some extent by the BCMS and the BCM programme.

The vast majority of organisations exist to provide products, services or both, so the Standard's emphasis on these is not unreasonable. On the other hand, financial threats, for example, could also pose risks to the organisation's ability to continue delivering products or services.

A company might supply a certain product to a major customer, as well as some smaller ones. If the major customer stopped demanding that product, this could result in the organisation then not being able to supply the product to the smaller customers, because of cost escalation or component shelf-life. In that case, the risk is not truly operational in nature, but it would, nonetheless, have an adverse impact on the continued provision of products.

Each organisation should decide upon its scope for BCM and for risk identification in this context. Importantly, the inclusion of non-operational risks should not mean that its BCMS cannot meet the requirements of good practice and of the Standard.

Custom and practice

In the context of business continuity, we are dealing principally with the organisation's ability to execute its normal functions in an operational sense – its operational risks. Other risks, strategic, commercial or business, that are also vulnerable to threats, are less likely to fall within the scope of BCM, but, most importantly, the BCM policy should set out which risks are being controlled wholly, or in part, by BCM.

ISO22301 defines risk as 'effect of uncertainty on objectives', but does go on to add that it is often expressed as a combination of consequences and the associated likelihood.

If the occurrence is more likely, we consider the situation more risky. If the impact is greater, we also consider the situation more risky. We can, therefore, consider a risk as the product of likelihood and impact; this is widely adopted as a sound approach to risk assessment.

Threats

Threats are an essential component in risks as, without them, the risks do not really exist. In the process of identifying risks, we have already identified the principal threat; this can often lead to the assessment of similar threats, as well as other activities that are vulnerable to the same threat. This is one of the ways in which brainstorming sessions often work quite well.

What needs to be established about a given threat is how likely it is to occur – its **likelihood**. In the examples earlier in this chapter, we looked at percentages of likelihood and the application of these to a scale of 0 to 5. But any scale of likelihood can be used if desired; it is a question of balance between accuracy and the workload required to achieve it.

The risk matrix also featured earlier in this chapter, which uses likelihood and impact scales of 1 to 5, is widely used, because experience indicates that it achieves a reasonable balance. Scales of 1 (or 0) to 100 could be used, but they would result in a large matrix, and it is doubtful whether much would be gained from this approach.

In some cases, it may be appropriate to consider likelihood in forms other than percentage. The frequency of occurrence may be considered so, just as different forms of impact are considered. A similar approach may be taken with likelihood, as in Figure 15.

Scale	Name	%age	Frequency
5	Very high	25	More than once a year
4	High	5-25	Every year
3	Medium	1-5	Every 2-3 years
2	Low	0.2-1	Every 5 years
1	Very low	0.01-0.2	Every 10 or more years

Figure 15: A typical likelihood scale

There is no scientific relationship between the percentage and frequency levels. It is a matter of judgement for each organisation to set their own set of criteria, but the activity should provide objectivity, as every threat is being assessed in the same way. ISO27001 refers to ensuring that risk assessments are 'reproducible', and this concept should also apply to the BCMS risk assessment. In other words, if a risk assessment is repeated by someone else, it should give the same results as before.

Multiple threats

In some cases, an incident could be caused by one of a number of threats, or by a combination of them.

Example 4 uses the example of a large tree that is next to a small office building.

Example 4: Multiple threats

There is a risk that the tree might fall, putting the office building out of use for some time. But the reasons that the tree might fall are really the threats. These reasons might include: very strong winds, prolonged, heavy rain, disease, being felled by mistake, and being struck by a large vehicle.

Each of these threats would exploit the same vulnerability: the fact that the tree is wooded and rooted in the earth.

Here, we are looking at five separate risks, because the likelihood that any of these threats will materialise is likely to be different for each. However, we can also combine the probabilities associated with each threat, because the result is effectively the same.

The likelihood (L) that the tree will fall on the building can be expressed as:

$L = Lw + Lr + Ld + Lf + Lv$

where the suffixes represent each of the threats listed above (wind, rain, disease, felling, vehicle).

If the likelihood of each threat materialising were 2%, the likelihood of the tree falling would, therefore, be 10%. This is, of course, only relevant if the organisation, or some of its activities, are vulnerable to the tree falling.

On the other hand, if the tree could only fall if all of the threats were present, then the likelihood would be expressed as:

$L = Lw \times Lr \times Ld \times Lf \times Lv$

which, in this case, would be 0.00000032%.

The likelihood of this event occurring is below even the lowest level on the scale in Figure 15 (0.01-0.2%), so Example 4 would fall outside the scope of the risk assessment.

Risk assessment

To assess risks, therefore, we must assess the threats against the organisation and its activities, and the extent to which they are vulnerable to these threats.

The most, basic approach to risk assessment is simply to judge whether a situation is of high, medium or low risk. This is rather subjective, in most cases, as it depends, firstly, upon the view of an individual about how likely it is that something (the threat) will happen – in other words, the likelihood. Secondly, it depends upon the individual's assessment of what the impact of that threat is likely to be; this, whilst less subjective, is nonetheless open to a certain amount of judgement.

We have already looked at the definition of risk and the likelihood of a threat materialising. A similar approach is required for assessing impact. What is required here is a set of standardised assessment criteria, such as can be found in *Figures 5* and *6*.

The risk assessment process consists, in applying impact and likelihood scales against each identified risk, to result in a risk 'score'.

The risk matrix

Example 2, earlier, contained the commonly-used 5 x 5 risk matrix. Each square contains a numerical value, or 'score', the product of the impact multiplied by the likelihood.

We have seen how conveniently scales of 1 to 5, for example, can facilitate different ways of looking at both impact and likelihood, so that all risks can be compared with each other.

Figure 16 gives a tabular view of an example in which eight different risks have been assessed using a standard set of likelihood and impact criteria, with scales of 1 to 5.

Risk	Likelihood	Impact	Score
A	4	2	8
B	4	3	12
C	3	3	9
D	4	2	8
E	4	3	12
F	2	3	6
G	2	5	10
H	5	5	25

Figure 16: Assessed risks

Figure 17 shows the same results, sorted in order of their scores. So, it is then relatively easy to select the most serious risks, and deal with them.

Risk	Likelihood	Impact	Score
H	5	5	25
B	4	3	12
E	4	3	12
G	2	5	10
C	3	3	9
A	4	2	8
D	4	2	8
F	2	3	6

Figure 17: Assessed risks, prioritised

But, a more sophisticated way of presenting this information would be to continue the use of the risk matrix, which, without any colour coding, would look like *Figure 18*.

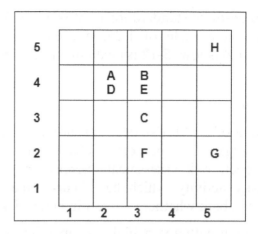

Figure 18: Risk matrix 1

Even in this format, we get a reasonable picture of which risks are the most severe, but, as we have seen earlier in the chapter, the use of coloured or patterned zones provides a much better visual representation, as in *Figure 19*.

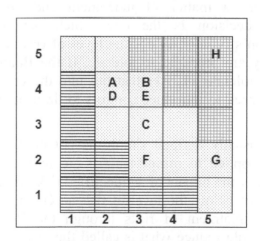

Figure 19: Risk matrix 2

There is no absolute standard for what is a low, medium or high score; on a scale of 1-25, it seems reasonable to suggest that 1-4 is low, 5-12 is medium and 13-25 is high.

Risk appetite

In the context of BCM, risk decisions are not usually about whether to engage in a particular activity, though in some cases a proper, risk assessment exercise may reveal an unduly, risky activity which has escaped management's attention, but about whether to invest in better risk controls.

An organisation with a very high risk appetite, would, after conducting its initial risk assessments, simply accept all the risks, as they are to save money on risk controls expenditure.

This risk matrix is one commonly used in risk management, though the 'grainy' diagonal risk bands of red, amber and green (the RAG classification), or the corresponding patterns, are a matter of judgement and choice. The important decision is the one which determines the organisation's risk appetite – the level of risk which, as a board, they are prepared to tolerate. If the Board decides that it can tolerate all risks that fall into the green area, it would not seek to introduce controls to limit the impact of those risks.

Controls (usually defined simply as countermeasures for risks) are applied to mitigate a risk, to reduce either the likelihood, or the impact of an identified risk, in such a way that it comes below the level of risk acceptance. In BCM terms, the treatment of risks through the BC planning process, should reduce what is called the residual risk (the risk that remains after treatment), to a level that is acceptable to the Board.

Interestingly, if one were to divide the three bands equally, or, at least, to the nearest whole number, so that low is 1-9, medium 10-17, and high 18-25, the resulting matrix would be as shown in *Figure 20*.

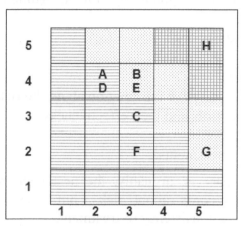

Figure 20: Risk matrix 3

In many respects, it does not matter where the red, amber and green zones are. What is important is, firstly, that risks with the same score should be treated in broadly the same way, and that, secondly, the Board approves the risk acceptance criteria.

Risk analysis

In most organisations, the use of the risk matrix described above will soon become impractical for individual risks, as more and more risks fall within the same square on the matrix. This is where the risk register, mentioned earlier in this chapter, becomes extremely useful.

The risk register is a widely used and accepted approach to risk management. It is a list of identified risks, with information about each, which may include:

- Nature of risk (including threat, vulnerability and impact)
- Likelihood
- Impact
- Risk score
- Findings – narrative information about the risk
- Current controls and their effectiveness
- Proposed controls
- Previous assessments.

The risk register is, arguably, the best way, not only of maintaining records about risks, but also of ensuring objectivity and consistency of treatment.

At a basic level, a risk register can simply be a list of risks, with associated assessments and scoring. It could be in the form of a spreadsheet, providing more functionality in terms of calculating, sorting and filtering data. At higher levels, it could be a powerful IT application capable of generating complex and comprehensive reports, and, perhaps, modelling data to determine optimum risk control activity.

An example of a spreadsheet-based risk register can be found in *Appendix 3*.

The risk register should be capable of some simple analysis to enable the prioritising risks for control, and to provide information for reporting purposes, so that the governing body is made aware of the organisation's risk exposure.

Risk control and treatment

Having identified and assessed all of the risks that fall within the defined scope, and, possibly, created a risk register, the organisation is presented with a reasonably, comprehensive picture of how exposed it is to operational risks, and business interruption risks in particular.

It is a good idea to develop a policy in respect of risks, so that resources for controlling them can be applied in a systematic way.

Having decided upon its risk acceptance criteria, and a classification of, say, high, medium and low (risks that are below the risk acceptance threshold), the policy could be as follows:

- Red risks must be reduced by way of controls within three months, so that they become amber (or green) within six months.
- Amber risks must be reviewed monthly and their controls (if any) also reviewed for effectiveness.
- Green risks must be reviewed every six months to ensure that they have not moved above the risk acceptance threshold.

Risk controls are simply measures that can be implemented in order to reduce the likelihood, or impact, of an event. They could be something as simple as a written procedure aimed at preventing mistakes, or something much more physical, for example, a flood-prevention or automatic fire-extinguishing system.

Risk controls may also be financial in nature, such as the insurance policies mentioned earlier in this chapter, or provisions in the profit and loss account.

The '4 Ts' approach to risk management controls uses the words: Tolerate – Treat – Transfer – Terminate.

Apart from the dubious credibility of lists of things that all begin with the same letter, one should also consider the practicality of these options. This approach is mentioned here more to acknowledge that it exists, than to promote it.

Clearly, if a risk is deemed intolerable, then 'tolerating' it is, at best, counter-intuitive. At the other end of the scale, 'termination' really means terminating the activity, rather than the risk; this may, in exceptional circumstances, be appropriate, but, generally, some control or treatment is likely to be the appropriate response.

Few organisations have either the budgetary capacity, or the management resource, to be able to control every single risk, and there must always be a level of tolerance of risks.

Preventative and curative measures

The adage 'prevention is better than cure', is generally true, but there are, of course, a great many threats in existence. Preventing them all from occurring is beyond the resources of the vast majority of organisations.

Some threats or incidents can be prevented – for example, the use of a firewall to prevent an attack on the IT system.

Such controls are called preventative controls. But other situations require a curative, or corrective, response, should they happen. Let's look at the example of a food manufacturing company (*Example 5*).

Example 5: Food manufacturer

This company uses a large quantity of mains water, on an almost continuous basis. Historically, the water supply has always been there, apart from the odd incident where some maintenance or construction work has interrupted the supply for a short time.

But, if the water supply were to be cut off for several weeks, the company simply could not operate, and would sustain an enormous financial impact.

There are a number of reasons why the supply could be cut for a prolonged period, and, in many circumstances, it may be possible to procure water in other ways.

The company's strategy now includes the potential use of a mobile water services provider. These companies are licensed to draw mains water from around the UK, and often provide this type of service for major events, where a mains supply does not exist.

In the event of the food manufacturer's normal mains supply being cut off, a mobile water services provider could supply, by tanker, sufficient water to keep the manufacturer going.

It would take some time, perhaps a couple of days, to establish this interim supply, but the company's BCP is now built around that knowledge.

The planning process also includes some minor modifications to the water pipework, so that, should it be required, the mobile supply could be connected without delay.

This is a curative (or corrective) control which would incur some cost if invoked, but this additional cost may well be covered by business interruption insurance, and, in this case, would be very much less than the eventual financial impact of letting customers down.

The risk management process

In simple terms, risk management involves:

1 Identification
2 Description and classification
3 Recording
4 Assessing
5 Application of mitigating controls
6 Management review
7 Reporting.

We have already looked at the first five of these elements, which may be described as the 'active' parts of the process. However, the majority of organisations, and all those seeking certification under ISO22301, also require a management review and assurance process, which is referred to in *Chapter 2*.

CHAPTER 4: BUSINESS CONTINUITY STRATEGY

BC strategy essentially means the identification of how the organisation is going to continue to meet the needs, and expectations, of its customers, clients or other stakeholders, in the event of some interruptive situation.

ISO22301 focuses on the protection, stabilisation and resumption of prioritised activities, which is fine if the direct resumption of an activity is a viable strategy, however, where the nature of the activity(ies) is such that meeting customers' needs in the shorter term is best done in other ways, then some interpretation of the Standard's requirements will be necessary.

In some respects, this chapter is an extension of the DR resource analysis in *Chapter 3*. There are some resources which can be replaced relatively easily, and others which cannot. It's worth remembering here that the Standard assumes that all activities are capable of being recovered, or restored, within the RTO. In this chapter, we are also going to look at strategies for activities that simply could not be treated in this way.

IT disaster recovery

The DR industry provides replacement resources for many types of organisation, as long as what they do is essentially to process information. They have people who sit at desks and use computers and telephones.

Office space, desks, chairs, personal computers (PCs) and telephones, are all generic tools which are used by the majority of organisations, and which can be obtained in a variety of different ways, at relatively short notice. They also require little customisation, to suit the individual organisation's needs.

For the type of organisation that uses only these ITDR resources, BC strategy should be relatively straightforward.

It is to be assumed that, should it be interrupted, every organisation with the slightest interest in this subject would wish to resume what it does. From this point, it becomes a matter of analysing the MTPD, or RTO, for each activity, as discussed in *Chapter 3*.

This process results in a resource timeline, similar to the activity recovery timeline in the previous chapter. This is a fairly simple process which can be executed manually, depending upon the complexity and size of the organisation. However, many activities that have a particular resource available to them, might be able to continue functioning without that resource for a period of time, so the RTO of the resource can be longer than the MTPD or RTO for the activity.

Ideally, the difference between the two, the 'resource tolerance', should be captured, along with other relevant information about the activity. The resulting resource timeline might look something like the example for IT applications in *Figure 21*.

Resource	RTO	RPO
E-mail	2D	2H
File server	2D	1D
Internet	2D	N/A
Database	2D	1D
MRP	2D	1H
HR system	14D	2D
Payroll	14D	2D

Figure 21: Resource timeline

RPO (recovery point objective) refers to the time point at which data should be restored to the application in question. Depending upon the nature of the organisation, its products and services, and any regulatory or customer requirements, RPO may be in days, hours, or even minutes.

This information should then enable the support service providers, such as IT, HR or facilities management, to establish contingencies against these timescale and recovery point requirements. Because the activity owner has expressed resource utilisation in terms of what is used, rather than how it is achieved, the support service provider can then arrange contingencies that will deliver the required resource.

A classic example of this is in IT applications. Ideally, users will state a requirement in terms of an IT application, as opposed to a particular server and other infrastructure.

They would also state the requirement for user terminals, such as PCs, also in as generic terms as possible.

Availability

Disaster recovery services are often marketed as 'availability' or 'high availability' solutions. They do pretty much what their name suggests – make things available in a time of need. However, the cost and actual availability should be considered carefully – a very good reason to conduct a BIA.

The fact is that generic resources, such as servers, PCs and office space, can be acquired reasonably easily in the marketplace. Of course, we have to gamble that the things we need will be available exactly when required, which is one of the key reasons that the ITDR industry exists. DR providers generally give a level of assurance that the necessary resources will be available when required, though this is almost never guaranteed. Most DR providers' contractual terms and conditions refer to 'best efforts', or 'best endeavours', in respect of the obligation upon them to provide the IT equipment, space and support services described in the contract.

If the BIA suggests that resources are not actually required immediately, but only after, say, three days, then one could speculate that it would be possible, in those three days, to find some serviced, office accommodation, buy some IT equipment, and get the organisation's activities running again within the RTO.

But, it's a gamble. The ITDR industry naturally wants everyone to think that it's too much of a gamble, and to believe that, in fact, the only reason that the required resources would not be available from them, would be because someone else got there first.

Some larger organisations have their own exclusive, virtually guaranteed, DR facilities. There are examples of stand-by 'hot sites', for the exclusive use of one organisation; but very few organisations can justify this level of availability.

Within the outsourced ITDR sector there are three fairly standard levels of availability (*see Figure 22*)

Availability	Resources provided	Recovery requirements
Cold site	Space: Seats (desks, etc.) IT hardware Telephones	Server builds Application installation Desktop build/configure Data restore Test and handover
Warm site	Items above, plus: Built servers Possibility of installed applications Possibility of configured desktops (PCs)	Application installation Data restore Test and handover
Hot site	Items above, plus: Applications installed in servers Configured desktops Possibility of replicated (live) application data Possibility of configured telephone switch/call management system	Data restore Test and handover

Figure 22: Standard levels of availability

Failover

This term refers to higher levels of availability for systems should they fail, usually offering continued access, not only to systems, but also to data. Failover amounts to another system automatically taking over from a failed 'master' system, so that there is little, or even no, interruption to system availability.

The ITDR marketplace

In the UK, the ITDR marketplace has become fairly polarised in the past five years, with a small number of large corporations having acquired their smaller competitors, so that the field of choice is now relatively narrow. This sector undoubtedly provides a very necessary service to the many organisations which could not reasonably create these types of contingencies for themselves.

ITDR providers achieve this by syndicating the resources they have, using a 'retainer and right to use' model, so-called because they are generic, and can be used by the majority of organisations.

Reciprocal and co-operative arrangements

For some organisations, the possibilities exist for setting up arrangements, whereby resources could be made available at another office or site within the organisation, or by another organisation. This latter approach is fairly uncommon, not least because of the competitive pressures between commercial organisations. However, there are some examples, particularly in the professional services and public sectors.

At the same time, this concept also represents a fairly common trap that many organisations fall into. It is tempting to say simply that, if Office A were unavailable, the staff could simply be transferred to Office B. This 'plan' is often based on untested and invalid assumptions, because it is unlikely that Office B will have the space, desks and IT equipment for everyone from Office A.

In many cases, however, a plan like this can be properly formulated. It could include arrangements for staff from Office B to be displaced, perhaps to work at home (the assumption that they would then be able to access the IT network would then need to be tested), or even from a customer's or client's premises.

Organisations that have more than one site can also consider building 'resilience' into their IT networks and data storage, where maintaining IT equipment on multiple sites is a feasible option. In some cases it is possible, not only to make alternative systems available if the main system should fail, but also to store back-up data in these, or similar systems, as opposed to the more traditional method of using tapes stored in a safe or off-site archive.

Go out and buy it

Many BCM practitioners express horror at such an idea, but for many organisations this can be a legitimate strategy for some, or even all, resources.

Computers, furniture and temporary accommodation are available in the market and, if one can set out a sensible plan based on what is likely to be available at any given time, then this can also be a very cost-effective strategy.

The ITDR market really provides the sort of availability required by many financial institutions, and others, where core activities must be up and running again within a day or less. But for organisations with longer MTPDs and RTOs, the acquisition of serviced, office accommodation and suitable off-the-shelf IT equipment, may well be possible within a number of days, or perhaps a week.

Some research of the IT equipment market would quickly reveal the likely delivery times for the hardware, and any software licences that might be required. Provided there is a reasonable range of suppliers, most of whom generally have stocks of the required products, then a list of these, with the appropriate detail, could prove to be a quite robust contingency plan.

In these cases, as with ITDR services, each organisation must make its own judgement as to how likely it is that the resources will be available when needed.

The go-out-and-buy-it strategy may also be a suitable, or indeed the only, approach for other resources, such as industrial plant or stocks of materials.

As we shall see later, there are also many situations where resources simply could not be replaced in anything like the RTO or MTPD, and where, once again, different strategies would be required.

People

BCM and, before it, DR, seem largely to have always assumed that organisations will not be deprived of this most important resource. It has to be said that, because many organisations have a number of people, compared with having one building, or one IT room, or one factory, the people resource is generally thought to be more resilient than the rest. The threat of an influenza pandemic, however, brings the dependency on people in the context of BCM into focus. The strategic options for replacing people are, in reality, extremely limited, except in some cases where agency staff could be used.

Here, the strategy may have to be much more about adjusting how the organisation operates if it loses some of its critical people.

The rest of the resource spectrum

So far, we have considered the strategic options for organisations whose activities are largely information processing or, at least, are achieved with the sort of generic resources described above.

But what about manufacturing companies, hotels, logistics and distribution businesses, or even schools and hospitals?

There is virtually no DR provision for them, except for their IT systems. This is where the Standard, which arguably grew out of the financial services industry, somewhat sidesteps the issue. The code of practice (Part 1) refers to the following resource types:

- People
- Premises
- Technology
- Information
- Supplies

- Stakeholders.

The only one of these that comes close to addressing this type of organisation is 'supplies', but there is little in this section of the Standard to indicate what is expected.

A BCMS cannot be complete, or comprehensive, if it does not provide for other operational aspects of the organisation, so strategies should be developed in respect of these resources, or, perhaps more appropriately, for the activities that depend upon them.

In manufacturing, for example, much of the resource base is bespoke, special purpose, or simply not available on a replacement basis within the sort of timescale that might be required.

There are other resources that might fall into the same generic category as those provided by the ITDR industry, such as vehicles, and some industrial plant and equipment. All the same, it would seem that the 'retainer and right to use' model, adopted by the ITDR industry, has not found favour in these other areas, where a more conventional hire market generally exists.

It should also be noted that the possibilities for rapidly replacing operational resources for organisations that do things other than process information, are generally quite limited. To address this set of issues, we must look again at what BCM is for.

BCM objectives

The beginning of this chapter suggests that BCM is there to ensure that the organisation meets the expectations of its customers, or other stakeholders, in the event of an interruptive incident. In fact, the Standard is really about restoring the critical activities that support key products and services. This implicit objective does not seem to take into account the value of business interruption insurance products.

A typical manufacturing company may well have more than enough business interruption insurance cover, so that any loss of profits resulting from production being interrupted would be met by this insurance. If that company were supplying some sort of commodity product, then customers might not be inconvenienced by such an interruption; in this case there would probably be little or no damage to the company's reputation. As soon as it was ready to reinstate its supplies into the market in question, the demand would remain and the company would continue to supply as before.

But for a great many products, and the vast majority of services, customers would be inconvenienced and, in many cases, incur losses as a result of the interruption to supplies. In the absence of any other arrangements, they might be forced to seek alternative supplies, and would then no longer demand what the company had previously supplied. Business interruption insurance typically does not cover this type of loss.

This is the scenario where the customer is let down by the supplier, even though it may not be the supplier's fault, and it can often lead to the customer making a positive decision not to buy from that supplier again. It may well be the case that the new supplier does not have any BCM arrangements in place, but that does not help the manufacturer who has just lost a customer. The customer held an expectation that the supplier would continue to supply products and would not let the customer down.

Many companies are nervous about discussing with their customers the possibility that something could go wrong, even though the vast majority of purchasing professionals know very well that no supply chain is 100% guaranteed. But if BCM is discussed with customers, their expectations can ultimately be modified, and a range of options can be examined.

The point here is that even if the only option is that supplies to the customer are simply suspended in the event of an interruptive incident, the customer would have effectively 'signed up' to that option, and its expectation would be met. That is a **strategy**.

Deliverables

A key feature of all management systems is that the thinking that has gone into it is visible and therefore documented.

As well as a strategy document being the sort of evidence a certification assessor would be looking for, it is also the most logical way of ensuring consistency in the development of the system, and continuity, as people within the organisation change.

The strategy document, or documents, will need to address the following:

- Ways of protecting activities against the effect of interruptive incidents; though these are likely, also, to exist as controls in the risk assessment and management section.

- Strategies for activities that can be viably resumed and for those that cannot.
- Information about the resources, interdependent activities, and other sources of help that might be relied upon, including:
  - People
  - Information systems and information itself
  - Other operating equipment and systems
  - Physical infrastructure
  - Transportation, including of people
  - Finance, for example for replacing stock, or rent for short-term workspace
  - Other organisations, including BaU, and emergency suppliers/providers
- Ways of reducing the associated risk – again likely also to exist as controls in the risk assessment and management section.

CHAPTER 5: BUSINESS CONTINUITY PROCEDURES

BC procedures were referred to by BS25999 as BCM response, and in many respects, this is what BCM is all about. The response that is executed in the event that something goes wrong, is based upon all of the analysis, preparation and planning that we have looked at so far.

The quality of the response will determine whether the impact actually sustained is within the limits that the governing body has accepted.

The requirements of the Standard are:

- An incident response structure (referred to at the beginning of *Chapter 5*), including communication mechanisms
- Business continuity and incident management plans
- Plans to restore business activities from temporary measures adopted.

The previous standard also specifically required that the BCM response is based on the outputs from determination of strategy, though it can probably be assumed now that to do otherwise would be so counter-intuitive that the rest of the system would be unlikely to meet the requirements of ISO22301.

The incident response structure

In a significant departure from BS25999's approach, incident response structure is essentially a set of processes for:

- Detecting incidents
- Establishing whether their severity warrants a formal BCM response
- Activating the response, including communications
- Availability of resources to enable the response to be executed.

Command structure – teams and roles

ISO22301 deals with the make-up and activities of the response team(s) in three sub-sections (8.4.2 – 8.4.4), however, this chapter continues to address these two facets together. When, and if, it comes to certification under the Standard, there are evidence requirements within the three sub-sections relating to response structure and to business continuity plans, which are covered in detail here.

In terms of command structure, the requirements depend entirely on the size and nature of the organisation. One of the lessons learned by a major, financial services company, from the 1996 bomb in Manchester, UK, was the importance of a well-designed, well-informed and capable leadership.

A very common pitfall in this area is to simply replicate the organisation's management structure, and, worse still, to use peoples' day job titles within the command structure.

Roles within the command structure need, really, to reflect the nature of the situation. So, for example, 'Team Leader' is often a more useful title than 'Chief Executive', not least because, in some situations, the best person to lead the command structure might not be the Chief Executive. Similarly, the Chief Executive might be the preferred media spokesperson for the organisation, but if he or she were to move on, the Marketing Director might then become the preferred spokesperson, rather than the new Chief Executive.

The key principles behind the command structure approach are listed below.

- Decision making in a crisis is very difficult, and is probably a completely new experience for the majority of executives, as there is virtually no opportunity to practise. In such a situation, it is arguably more important than ever that, regardless of whether the organisation's day-to-day management is team based or hierarchical, those making decisions have the benefit of contact with senior colleagues, with whom to arrive at the best decisions for the organisation.

- Decisions made in respect of one part of an organisation can have an effect on other parts of it. If the entire organisation is represented in the decision-making process, those decisions are likely to be better overall.

- In a crisis, it may be that some parts of the organisation are required to make compromises, or even sacrifices, in order that another part may continue to operate or recover. Any significant conflicts that such a decision may create are probably best handled at the most senior level, so that implementation of such decisions can be rapid, in what is bound to be a very fast-moving environment.

Teams and structure

Many organisations need no more than a single team, comprising members whose roles reflect the various departments or divisions that execute the organisation's critical activities, and those that provide support services to those departments, such as IT, facilities management, human resources management, industrial services, health and safety, security, and so on.

This may work well for smaller organisations based on a single site, but, as organisations get larger in terms of corporate structure, numbers of staff and location, the need for a structure of teams is likely to emerge.

In order to establish what sort of team structure might be required, it is worth looking at what tasks members of these teams actually need to undertake.

The principal tasks include:

- Collecting information about the incident, impacts and the progress of recovery activities
- Taking decisions
- Implementing decisions
- Directing critical activities in recovery
- Communicating, both internally and externally.

A single team is probably desirable, but each member of that team will need direct communications with at least one other member of the relevant department, or division, who can execute decisions made by the team and report back on progress. Depending upon the size of the organisation, that person might be the leader of another team, and that team might, in its turn, need to convene, in order to agree decisions in a similar way to the first team. This could be the case if decisions taken by the first team can be implemented in a number of ways; it depends on how 'strategic' those decisions are.

A two-tier structure thus emerges, though this should be based upon need, rather than anything else; there is no merit in two organisations trying to make decisions that subsequently conflict with each other.

One of the more popular approaches is the 'Gold, Silver and Bronze' structure, adopted by the emergency services in the UK for civil emergency management, though this title is really little more than a familiar labelling of a three-tier arrangement.

Example 6 shows how this might be applied in other settings. It relates to a medium-large company engaged in an information-processing type of business, comprising a number of subsidiary companies, operating at a variety of locations.

Example 6: Gold, Silver and Bronze

This company comprises three or four subsidiaries of a holding company, which, itself, takes a minimal form. The Group Chief Executive is also Chief Executive of the largest subsidiary, and the other subsidiaries have their own Chief Executives. The group's companies are generally distributed separately, so that most of its offices are dedicated to one company or another, but the group will, sensibly, make use of these offices in the event that one of them, particularly the largest, is unavailable. Each subsidiary could simply have its own single team, but there are scenarios which would require a group level response, such as pandemic influenza, or a major reputational incident, so there is a Gold team which operates at group level, as well as a Silver team for each subsidiary. The size of the subsidiaries is such that Bronze teams for each of the support functions, for example, are not necessary, and the Silver team will utilise the existing management in those areas to execute its decisions. The group's IT systems are managed at group level, providing a service to each of the subsidiaries, and there is a Bronze team responsible for this part of the response and recovery process ...

Example 6 continued

... The Bronze IT team has 'relationships' with the Gold team and with each of the Silver teams. If the incident is confined to one location, the Gold team may not be convened, unless, perhaps, there were a fatality, or something of that severity, and the Bronze IT team would simply work with the relevant Silver team to restore critical activities. If there were a pandemic or some scenario likely to affect multiple subsidiaries, the Gold team would be convened and take the majority of the decisions.

This mechanism is written into the BCP, so that it is clear how the structure will work in a variety of situations.

In other organisations, the Gold team may need to take all the strategic decisions, such as what stories to release to the media, or whether to suspend operations. This leaves the Silver team to get on with the job of restoring critical activities.

Roles

Put simply, the roles within a team need to reflect the sort of tasks that are likely to be required. Appendix 4 provides an example of a Crisis Management Team and its roles.

Collecting information

The command team(s) cannot take effective decisions if they do not know what is actually going on. In order to establish the nature and extent of an incident, it may be appropriate to appoint one or more roles tasked with reporting to the command structure.

An important planning consideration for roles such as this, is the provision of appropriate communication facilities and channels. These might include mobile telephones, two-way radios, and forms designed to prompt the collection of relevant information.

Communicating with stakeholders

Telling people what is going on is an obvious thing to do, when one considers incident management in the cold light of day. In the event of a real incident, however, people may be under such pressure that informing others of the situation starts to get forgotten.

An obvious way of addressing this is to include, in the command structure, at least one role focused almost entirely on external communications.

Team resilience – deputies

In day-to-day situations, people in decision-making roles may, from time to time, be absent. It is not practical, in a crisis situation, to wait for that person to return, and it is unlikely that the sort of control and decision making required can be achieved remotely, even using such facilities as video conferencing.

An important feature of the command structure is deputisation. Some roles may require more than one deputy, particularly where the nominees for those roles habitually travel away from the operational base(s).

It may be natural for the Chief Executive or Managing Director to take major decisions on responding to a crisis, so, in identifying deputies for command structure roles, it is critical to ensure that these deputies would be capable of leading and taking decisions, or of simply executing the tasks that might be required.

As we shall see later, exercising is a key factor in the success of the command structure. As well as reading a description of what they would have to do, the capability of people who would be expected to perform roles in the command structure will be enhanced if they have the opportunity to practise it on a reasonably, regular basis.

Triggering the BCM response – activation

The command structure should be the means by which the BCM response is activated, and it is important to identify who has the authority to do that.

This would usually be the leader of the command structure or crisis management team, or it might be someone more senior, depending upon how the teams and roles were structured.

Typically, the activation authority would formally end the business continuity phase and stand the command structure down once stable interim operations, or whatever level of recovery is stipulated in the plan, had been achieved.

The Standard requires the following:

1 An impact threshold that justifies a formal response – this could simply be a descriptive narrative providing guidance to anyone authorised to initiate, such as:
   'The command team leader may initiate a formal response when any incident or situation, in his/her judgement, is likely to result in operational interruption of half a day or more, or an equivalent impact according to the impact table within the BIA.'

2 Assessment of the nature and extent of an incident – in many cases this can quite easily be incorporated in the statement above.
3 Activation of the response – again, easily covered by the above statement.
4 Processes and procedures for activation – these would normally be an integral part of a business continuity plan, but may, if preferred, be a separate document, or set of documents.
5 Arrangements for communication with interested parties, authorities and media – again these are typically embodied in a business continuity plan.

Wherever these arrangements exist, their existence would normally mean that the specific requirements of the Standard are met, however, for certification purposes, it would make sense to record against the Standard, where in the management system's documentation, specific requirements are placed.

Business continuity planning

The business continuity plan, the BCP, is arguably the ultimate deliverable in a BCM project. It provides the basis for the command structure's decision making, and therefore, how the organisation responds to, and recovers from, the incident or interruption.

As we have seen already, the BCP should be based on the organisation's objectives, the RTOs, and upon valid assumptions regarding the availability of resources with which critical activities may be recovered.

For this reason, business continuity planning comes towards the end of the BCM development project, rather like an executive summary.

Policy, strategy and objectives have all been dealt with elsewhere in the BCMS, so these are things that really do not need to be in the BCP, which should be telling the organisation's command structure how to respond to the situation it finds itself in, and how to recover from it.

A BCP can be in a variety of formats. To be of practical value, though, it should be as simple as possible. In a fast-moving and stressful situation, even the most rehearsed and experienced team should not be concerned with how or why the BCMS has been developed, or, indeed, that it is based upon the principles of ISO22301!

Master plan

Regardless of the nature of an incident, the organisation's recovery objectives should be the same, and should form a focal point in the master plan. Equally, the command structure, whilst it should be capable of dealing with a wide variety of different scenarios, should be based upon a core team. An effective master plan is likely to include the sections below.

Summary

A clear statement setting out the purpose of the BCP, that it forms the basis for the command team, or structure, to make decisions and lead response and recovery activities, and the circumstances and scope under which it should be used or followed.

Activation

A statement of who is authorised to activate the BCP, effectively triggering the BCM response. As we have seen, this is likely to be the leader of the command structure or team, and should include one or, preferably, more than one, deputy. The master plan, like everything else in the BCMS, will be subject to regular review and updating, so stating the names of the individuals who are authorised to activate the plan is a sensible idea, eliminating ambiguity in what could well be a very, stressful situation.

Lessons have been learned by many organisations faced with a major incident or crisis, where there were serious delays in triggering the BCM response, because it was not possible to contact the one person who could authorise activation of the plan.

Command location

Similarly, lessons have also been learned by some organisations which wasted a lot of valuable time trying to decide how and where to mobilise their command team.

It is not difficult to work out, and decide, a number of locations where the command team(s) could be based. The choice of location should take into account:

- Availability 24-hours a day, seven days a week
- Suitability for lengthy, group-working sessions
- Communications:
  - Land lines
  - Mobile phone signal(s)
  - Internet services
  - Telephones and fax machines

- Distance and travel time from the site(s) in question
- Availability of rest and catering facilities
- Permanent, secure storage facilities for 'battle box' and similar essential items.

For some scenarios, such as pandemic flu, the logical command location is often the organisation's headquarters, and this should be included in the list of command locations, if appropriate, as should others which would not be affected by site-specific incidents, such as fire, flood or explosion.

If a command location is owned by a third party, there should be adequate assurance and knowledge that the location is likely to be available, with suitable alternatives should this prove not to be the case. One local hotel, for example, with no alternative location, is unlikely to be sufficiently robust.

Command structure

Covered earlier in this chapter, the master plan is a good place to set out details of the command structure, team or teams. Detailed lists of duties and responsibilities, should they be necessary, are probably best attached as appendices, so that the plan remains concise and, therefore, highly practical.

For each team, a list of the roles, together with the names of the person assigned to that role and of the deputies, should provide a sufficient level of detail for the majority of organisations, as in *Figure 23*.

Role	Responsible	1st Deputy	2nd Deputy
Leader	Alison Bond	Charles Davis	Eric Finch
Health and safety/security	Graham Harris	Ian Jones	Karl Lewis
ICT	Martin Norris	Oliver Penson	N/A
Facilities	Quentin Roberts	Sarah Thomas	N/A
Customer services	Una Villiers	Will Young	N/A
Sales	Amanda Chambers	Barry Dawson	Colin Evans
Manufacturing	Diane Foster	Eddie Gray	N/A
Logistics	Frank Hinton	Gordon Ivers	N/A
Finance	Charles Davis	Eric Finch	N/A
Human resources	Ian Jones	Sarah Thomas	N/A
Media and communications	Helen James	Barry Dawson	Alison Bond

Figure 23: A command team

Priorities and objectives

The organisation's recovery objectives have been established through the BIA, and should be stated here. It may also be appropriate to state other objectives and priorities, such as:

- **Personal safety** – that the safety of all people will come before the recovery of business activities, or the protection of property. ISO22301 states that life safety should be the first priority in incident response.
- **Welfare** – that the organisation will treat the welfare of all its staff and, possibly, any visitors directly affected by the incident, as a priority, and will, or may, provide resources to support this.
- **Reputation** – whilst it may seem obvious that any organisation needs to recover its critical and other activities, as soon as possible, it may, in some cases, be even more important that actions are taken to protect the organisation's reputation through media statements, PR activity, person-to-person communications, or the like.
- **Security** – some organisations may be exposed, in certain circumstances, to attacks on property, in such forms as:
  - Looting
  - Fraud
  - Money laundering
  - Vandalism
  - Theft of mail or goods in transit.

These priorities should be articulated in the master plan, as well as being included in more detailed plans.

Scenario plans

In the earlier days of business continuity, many practitioners suggested that, because recovery priorities should be the same, regardless of the nature of the interruption, scenario-based plans were inappropriate and represented an unnecessary duplication of information. Nowadays, however, the range of potential situations that most organisations face is so broad, that to have one plan that deals with everything is usually completely impractical.

Let us consider two examples: a premises-related incident, such as a major fire, and pandemic flu.

A major fire is more likely to occur at night, or when the premises are empty. In 2005, deaths caused by fires in buildings other than dwellings, were less than one per 1,000 fires, and non-fatal casualties were only 40 per 1,000 fires (*Fire Statistics, United Kingdom, 2005 Department for Communities and Local Government: London, March 2007*). The emphasis, therefore, must be on recovering critical activities as quickly as possible, predicated upon the likely availability of the organisation's staff.

In the case of pandemic flu, on the other hand, it will be the people who are unavailable, and so the response cannot generally be about restoring activities as quickly as possible.

Typically, scenario plans work well as a subset of the master plan. They enable the command teams, or structure, to focus on the type of response required for the scenario in question, without the unnecessary confusion of responses to other, quite different, scenarios.

Depending on what the organisation does, the range of scenarios might include:

- Premises incidents – including fire, flood, explosion and structural damage.

- Denial of access – where systems in the premises may still be operational, but, for safety or security reasons, people are not allowed in, or near, the premises.
- Resource failures – typically including IT and telecommunications, as well as utilities, supplies, transport and, perhaps, people.
- Malicious acts – including terrorism-related incidents, sabotage, breaches in information and physical security.
- Pandemic – whilst this may fall into the resource failures (people) category, there are some unique response actions likely to be required in the event of escalating World Health Organisation (WHO) pandemic alert phases.
- Environmental contamination.
- Reputational incidents.

The operational risk assessment (*see Chapter 3*) should identify the full range of interruption scenarios for each organisation. These should then be transferred into the BCM response phase of the programme.

Recovery plans

The master plan sets out, amongst other things, the RTO for many of the organisation's activities, as well as the minimum activity level in each case.

An organisation conducting only one or two activities could feasibly include the details for how those activities are to be recovered, but it is likely that, in the majority of cases, individual activity or process recovery plans will be required.

The activity recovery plans will typically set out a short narrative of how and where the activity should be recovered, and specific details, including:

- Primary and secondary (if planned) locations
- DR resources and how they are invoked
- Other resources, such as those normally used by other staff, and how they are obtained
- Contingencies for lower-than-expected levels of resource availability, including people
- Methods of communication
- Reporting requirements (to the command structure)
- Interim or alternative arrangements for travel, accommodation and shift patterns
- Reconciliation of information in use before the interruption with that which has been restored
- Dealing with backlogs of work.

These recovery plans should generally be 'owned' by the person responsible for managing, or leading the activity on a day-to-day basis, maximising the likelihood that they will actually work when used for real.

Other plan components

Effective execution of response and recovery tasks is also likely to be enhanced through the use of additional components, which may include those below.

Procedures

Procedures are essential for a variety of tasks that are likely to be required during the entire, business continuity phase. They will almost certainly be required for the invocation of

DR and other resources, providing important information about how to activate or invoke these resources, how they should be used, and what levels of performance, or activity, should be expected.

Procedures are also likely to be of great value for other activities that are not usually undertaken, such as communication cascades, media handling, infection control, casualty management, security, and many more.

Documented procedures will be required for the recovery, or restoration, of supporting resources including DR; for the recovery of critical and other activities; and for any other detailed tasks that might be required, such as arranging alternative supplies to customers.

Incident log

The value of keeping a reasonably, comprehensive record of an incident cannot be understated. BCM is an important component in corporate governance, as it provides some assurance that the organisation has taken appropriate steps to control, and minimise, the risks associated with, *inter alia*, business interruption. Similarly, any investigation into, or scrutiny of, the handling of an incident and recovery from it, will require the best, possible evidence that the organisation did, in fact, use its BC plan.

The inclusion of blank incident log sheets in the BCM system should ensure that the right information is recorded and that time is not wasted. It should also ensure that there is no failure to record early events because of the time taken before someone realised the need to keep a record.

5: Business Continuity Procedures

Internal communication

In many organisations, there is likely to be the need to inform staff of any incident, or similar situation, as quickly as possible, without occupying significant amounts of time for members of the command structure. The more traditional communication cascade, or calling tree approach, if well designed, can provide a good level of assurance that all the necessary people can be informed.

Some larger organisations are beginning to use the emerging notification services, of which there appears to be a growing number. With the very widespread use of 'smartphones' and other mobile devices, the use of these systems is becoming increasingly viable, and assuming that costs continue to fall, it can only be a matter of time before they are used in the majority of cases.

However, for the time being, the traditional methods remain of value to many organisations, and whilst a cascade system need not necessarily follow the organisation's management structure, there are obvious benefits in its doing so, as far as is practicable. Many organisational structures, however, do not make the best cascade structures, as they may involve senior people (who are more likely to be members of the command structure) in contacting a large number of people, when they may be urgently needed for leadership tasks.

A sensible approach is to start with the existing management structure. In *Figure 24*, a conveniently-balanced management structure provides the basis for an equally, well-balanced cascade system. Group 0 is effectively at the command team level. Some, or all, of its members are themselves leaders of Level 1 groups. Two members of Group 1 (Level 1) are leaders of Level 2 groups, and two members of Group 11 (Level 2) are leaders of Level 3 groups.

This example shows one deputy for every group, though, in some circumstances, a second deputy may be appropriate.

In larger organisations, the cascade structure may be very complex; individuals really only need to see the people that they are required to contact, including deputies, in the event that the leader of a group cannot be contacted.

A simple cascade, like that in *Figure 24*, is easy to use in this form, though it would, of course, require some contact information for each person. For much bigger structures, a different approach is likely to be needed. Appendix 5 contains an example of a spreadsheet-based cascade list, which is almost infinitely scalable.

The cascade system should also take into account the need to provide feedback to the command structure, and to request further information, or to request authority, for particular actions that might be appropriate at the time.

With this in mind, the leader of a cascade group cannot simply contact everyone on their list and then switch their phone off. Their role as a cascade leader may well need to include being able to receive calls from 'downstream'.

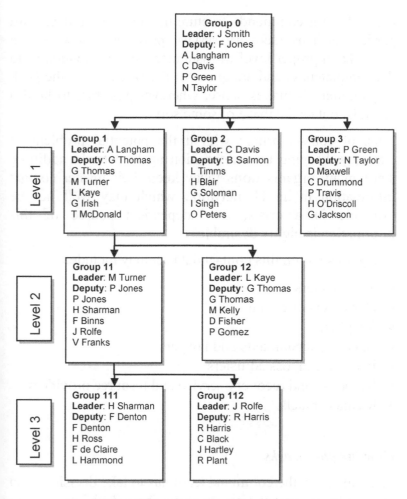

Figure 24: A cascade system

Contact data

When asked about contact data that might be needed in a crisis, most people simply hold up their mobile phone. This may well be a sensible component of the BCP, and provide the ability for command-structure members to contact third parties, such as recovery service providers. However, in order that a proper level of assurance can be provided as to the completeness and adequacy of the BCMS, and the BCP in particular, it makes sense, wherever possible, to hold a central, contact database of some sort.

This, of course, brings with it the potential problem of currency; keeping the information up to date. In addition, since many organisations today keep their master contact information in an IT network, which may well not be available in a crisis, an independent source of this information is highly desirable.

Categories within this contact data set may include:

- Stakeholders
- Customers or clients
- Suppliers
- Bankers, accountants and lawyers
- Insurers and loss adjusters
- Response and recovery service and resource providers
- Media contacts.

How the plan works

In a real crisis, the command team has to take decisions and execute them, usually very quickly. These decisions need to be informed, not only by the situation at the time, but also by a lot of common sense that has been fully thought through at a time when there was not a crisis.

The plan may be a single document that aims to deal with the majority of situations, or a multilevel system comprising a master plan and scenario plans. In either case, it should act as a set of decision-support tools identifying the overall theme of the response, or the approach to it, and likely actions that should be taken in reply to certain trigger events or times.

The plan should go on to identify specific procedures for tasks that would not typically be undertaken on a regular basis. These include the invocation of DR and other resources, communications with staff and stakeholders about the incident, the recording of key information about what happened, and the decisions taken by the command team(s), and the results of those decisions.

The command team(s) would generally work as a group, referring to the various levels of planning documentation, taking decisions, and then executing them through appropriate communication channels available at the time.

The typical evolution of a crisis is likely to include a number of phases, as in *Figure 25*.

During the **incident response** phase, a clear, concise plan is essential, together with more detailed procedures, or instructions, for executing decisions taken by the command team or structure. Movement into the recovery phase is likely to be characterised by the successful accounting for all people, and the satisfactory management of any casualties or fatalities. In situations involving contamination, such as CBRN, this phase is likely to continue until the safety of all staff and visitors has been assured.

The **recovery** phase is likely to follow the incident response phase immediately, but, in some situations, there could well be an overlap between the two. The command team(s), as in any crisis situation, will need to use their judgement regarding the commencement of recovery tasks before all health, safety and welfare issues have been fully resolved.

The recovery phase is primarily focused upon the deployment and invocation of contingency arrangements and alternative ways of working – the recovery of critical activities. Whilst, for many, this may mean picking up where they were before the incident, and continuing to do what they would normally do on a daily basis, the effects of an incident, even one that appears fairly minor, should not be underestimated.

The use of welfare resources, including counselling or flexible working arrangements, may well be appropriate. Documented recovery plans, with related procedures, will be important, particularly where some individuals are less capable of executing their normal, daily tasks than they would otherwise be.

The objective of most BCPs is likely to be to return much of the organisation to a stable, interim operational state, as quickly as possible, and to protect the organisation's brand and reputation. The latter will be achieved significantly through effective communication with clients, or customers, and any other influencers, including the media.

The media-handling component which is likely to be present in the incident response phase, will, therefore, probably continue into the recovery phase, perhaps shifting from a reactive to a proactive stance.

The **continuity** phase represents stability of the interim operational state, and may continue for some considerable time, depending on the nature of the incident and the organisation's infrastructure.

Incident	Hours	Days	Weeks

Incident response
Evacuation
Personal safety
Casualty management
Security
Media handling

Recovery
Deployment of command team(s)
Assessment and reporting
Activation of scenario plan(s)
Invocation of DR and other resources
Activation of recovery plans
Internal communications
PR and stakeholder communications
Recovery of activities to interim state

Continuity
Welfare and morale management
Increasing stability of activities
Salvage and asset recovery
Insurance claims processing

Criticality
10 9 8 7 6 5 4 3 2 1 0

Figure 25: Crisis evolution

Multilevel (organisational) plans

In larger organisations where there are multiple locations, entities, business units, companies, and so on, a multilevel plan structure may well be appropriate.

Such a structure will depend entirely upon the nature of the organisation in question, but the guidelines below should always be borne in mind:

- Less is more – the fewer plans, the better.
- Many incidents are location specific, and are best dealt with by a location-based plan, often regardless of the corporate structure within the location.
- Major issues that may affect the organisation's brand may be best handled at the highest level, with two, or even more, plans operating simultaneously.
- The command structure may change as higher, or lower, level plans are activated, and deactivated.

In practice, it is relatively difficult to achieve complete synchronisation between plans at different levels. What is often most important is that the rules for activation do not force a number of competing plans to be operating at the same time.

Ending the business continuity phase

It may seem obvious that, when the organisation or its component parts have reached an acceptable level of operational stability, the BCP and command structure should, at some point, be stood down.

In longer-term situations, where return to BaU is not possible, people get used to working in a different way, and the value of keeping the command structure in place will begin to diminish. In this type of situation, attention must soon turn to planning the return to whatever level of normality is possible.

In other situations, interim working may last for only a few weeks, or even days, and here it may well be appropriate to keep the command structure in place until BaU has been achieved and stabilised.

The BCP should refer to ending the business continuity phase, including the communications which should accompany that action. Stakeholders, customers, clients and staff will need to know when the whole thing is over and normal service can be expected.

In addition to this, many organisations may well be able to benefit from PR at this stage. Positive stories about organisations that survive a major interruption unscathed are quite rare, and if clients' and customers' expectations have been met, or even exceeded during the business continuity phase, there will be much to celebrate and capitalise upon.

Recovery

ISO22301 introduces a new requirement; there should be a plan to recover from the temporary arrangements adopted. The Standard is actually quite un-specific here; it doesn't require plans for returning to the business as usual state, nor does it suggest returning to the premises or other location affected by an incident. What it seems to be getting at is that there should be a way of resuming activities to the pre-incident level, and there are clearly a number of ways of meeting this requirement.

A procedure is whatever the organisation decides it should be; it could be anything between specific instructions for setting up parallel operations in another location, and a broad statement that the organisation will identify the best way to resume what it was doing before the incident, perhaps by way of a project.

The key issue here is that the starting point is somewhat unknown. What any organisation decides to do about longer term resumption of activities can vary widely, dependent upon the situation at the time.

It is unlikely that detailed plans to return to the pre-incident location(s) are worthwhile, not least because that may not be possible, and for a variety of reasons.

In larger, multi-site, organisations, a possible strategy post-incident is simply not to re-instate a particular operation, instead transferring its output to another unit. In others, it may make more sense to re-instate activities, but the way of doing that is likely to depend upon what has actually happened.

Ultimately, it is for the organisation to decide how much of a plan it can draw up for this requirement – the main gist of the Standard is to establish how customers' requirements or expectations would be met; that they may have put up with lower levels of output or supply, but there needs to be an understood way of meeting their longer term requirements.

CHAPTER 6: EXERCISING AND TESTING

A classic failing of a great many business continuity plans, is that they are written and then left on the shelf. People are usually amazed at how quickly their organisation changes and thus how quickly their plan becomes no longer operable as intended. There are also plenty of examples of organisations attempting to use plans in earnest, only to find that they are too difficult to follow, with the result that the leadership resorts to 'making it up as they go along'. This inevitably means that poor decisions are taken, and that the overall impact sustained is worse than expected.

ISO22301 quite rightly demands that BCM arrangements are reviewed regularly, are updated to reflect change, and are exercised from time to time, so that their operability is checked, and people involved in managing the BCM response have a chance to practise what they may have to do for real.

Exercises

This is an opportunity to demonstrate application of the PDCA model referred to earlier in the book. The Planning and Doing have been executed with the development of plans and contingencies, and their implementation, including awareness and training for people involved in managing the response. The exercise is an opportunity to test, or check, how practically feasible the response actually is. The record of what happened should subsequently be used to modify, or improve the plan and related arrangements, which is the Act part of the PDCA actions.

Planning the exercise

In an ideal world, an exercise would comprise complete simulation of a major incident, including shutting down systems, premises and critical activities, then invoking all of the contingency resources. It would also be allowed to run for as long as necessary to ensure completion.

Such an exercise would be the most rigorous test of all the assumptions, capabilities, availability and resource performance possible, but is unlikely ever to be carried out, because of the cost. In fact, ISO22301 states that exercises should '... minimise the risk of disruption of operations', and, whilst interrupting normal activities to conduct an exercise may not be an incident in itself, the result would be much the same. The Standard's predecessor, BS25999, also required that an exercise should not cause an incident, which is arguably a statement of the obvious, and in any case largely falls within the requirements of minimising disruption.

In most organisations, exercises are likely to take place only annually, so every opportunity should be taken to test as much of the BCM arrangements as possible.

Probably the most common exercise scenario in use is the fire, which is often also used to test fire evacuation performance.

The general objective is to set a scenario, including a major incident, and then see how the command structure and the organisation as a whole, respond. It is usually necessary also to accelerate the evolution of the business continuity phase in an exercise, so that what might normally take several days to happen, can be simulated during the course of half a day.

Of course, people would not actually be sent home, and customers, for example, would not be contacted. The exercise though, should include the decisions being taken to do all these things, but with their execution limited to within the boundaries of the organisation.

The overall objective for the exercise should be stated at the outset. It will be a matter of testing the content of plans, procedures and other documents, checking the availability and specification of contingency resources (including DR), and rehearsing the command team(s) in their execution of the BCM arrangements as a whole.

The decisions that may be executed during such an exercise could include:

- Evacuation of premises
- Convening command teams
- Testing deputisation in command teams
- Testing the cascade system(s)
- Testing deputisation in cascade systems
- Generating media and corporate communications statements
- Conducting simulated media interviews
- Testing IT disaster recovery (where available)
- Deploying small numbers of staff to alternative workplace locations
- Checking samples of contact information.

These activities should be designed to test the 'logic' of the plan and arrangements, and the behaviour of those involved in the process, to see whether those people appointed to particular roles or tasks behave in more or less the way expected and assumed.

Exercises generally require facilitation. There will need to be at least one person, external to the organisation's command structure, driving the accelerated timeline of the exercise, inserting conditions of further incidents, and helping to keep the team(s) focused on objectives.

The exercise plan can be a simple, one-page document describing the objectives, incident scenario, further incidents along the timeline, additional resources to be brought in to add realism or urgency, and requirements for recording what actually happens.

It may be desirable for the command structure to have limited or, indeed, no knowledge of the exact time the exercise will start, or of the scenario itself.

Generally, time should be allowed at the end of the exercise for debriefing, giving participants the opportunity to ask questions, seek clarification, and make suggestions as to how things could be improved. This is the best time to capture this sort of information; people are much less inclined to provide feedback later on.

Execution

The facilitator, or team, should simply inform a relevant person that the exercise has started, and tell them the nature of the incident.

If the exercise is the first for the organisation, due consideration should be given to how conversant, members of the command team(s) can realistically be with the BCM arrangements, and how the plan works. The exercise will be as much an opportunity for the organisation to learn how to operate its own BCM arrangements, as to test the specifics of resources, provisions and mechanisms.

In addition to the nominated person(s) maintaining the incident log(s), the facilitation team will probably benefit from a more comprehensive record of what is happening. In many cases, the use of video recording in the command location can be put to good effect.

In most organisations, the exercise will be time limited, so the facilitator will need to ensure that the planned evolution of the business continuity phase is achieved, and that there is time for a debrief at the end.

Reporting

Some time will be required immediately after the exercise, in which to analyse information recorded at the time. The key deliverables from an exercise will be:

- Lessons learned
- Changes needed – not only to components of the BCMS, but also to review frequencies where relevant
- Successes.

ISO22301 requires that a written report is produced, which should embody these key deliverables, with exercise records as appendices.

CHAPTER 7: PERFORMANCE EVALUATION

ISO22301 introduces standard terminology, consistent with other international management system standards, and whilst it no longer includes the rather important term 'review' from BS25999, it replaces this with a requirement to evaluate the business continuity procedures, together with the requirement to take corrective action when anything no longer conforms to requirements.

Monitoring and measurement

The case for continuously reviewing and maintaining the BCMS, particularly the executable parts of it, is already made. However, to ensure that this actually happens, the majority of organisations will benefit from establishing a review body.

Depending upon the nature of the organisation, regular review and maintenance of individual components, such as plans, procedures and contact information, will be conducted by a variety of people. One of the tasks of the review body should be to monitor this ongoing process of monitoring and measuring performance of operation, and testing of the BCMS.

Every executable component of the system should have an owner and a review status. This should mean that the owner is responsible for monitoring the item according to the stipulated review schedule.

The timely and competent review and maintenance of plans and resources should become a KPI in the reporting and assurance process (*see Chapter 11*). This is achieved relatively easily by way of a document register (*see Chapter 10*) that includes information on ownership and review.

Criteria

The first step in the overall improvement process is to decide what needs to be measured and therefore monitored.

Some key parameters for measurement are likely to include:

- Accuracy
- Timeliness
- Comprehensiveness
- Meeting of objectives
- Levels of awareness amongst staff and other stakeholders.

These are, of course, very general, but are likely to apply variously to features of the system, such as:

- Documents
- Contingency arrangements
- Plans and scenarios
- Measurement and monitoring activities, including exercises.

Meeting objectives is a measurement criterion that should probably always feature in a BCMS. Many certification auditors will expect to see some evaluation of whether the system is delivering what the Board have asked for; the objectives that are enshrined in, or referred to by, the policy.

Bearing in mind that BC arrangements generally only prove their ultimate worth in the event of an incident, demonstrating that all objectives are being met is, of course, a challenge.

This is where exercises may help; the report of an exercise may include an assessment of what the impact would have been had the incident, or scenario, been real; and this can then be compared with the impact limitation requirements within the BCM objectives.

Other objectives might include enhancing competitiveness, for example. Again, it is not easy to show that a new piece of business has been won, or lost, as a result of having a BCMS in place, and it will be for each organisation to work out how it can use the new resilience it has acquired as a competitiveness tool, and monitor its worth in that respect.

The BCMS

The BCMS itself should also be monitored, measured and evaluated on a regular basis, through internal audit and management review, as is common practice in other management systems. This process will typically include a mechanism for maintenance and improvement, through the recording and processing of preventive and corrective actions.

Internal audit

ISO22301 is not expansive on the requirements for internal audit. Those with knowledge or experience of other management systems will probably be familiar with procedures and systems in this area. Essentially, a documented procedure and audit plan will be required, setting out the criteria against which the BCMS should be audited, and a forward programme of audits, together with some evidence of previous planned audits having been completed.

The audit should focus on two aspects; that the BCMS continues to meet the organisation's requirements and those of ISO22301:2012, and that it is being properly implemented and maintained.

There should be an audit programme that features:

- Audit procedures, including criteria for judging conformance, reporting of non-conformance, and the resulting corrective action process.
- An audit plan, setting out scheduled audits at frequencies commensurate with the importance of the organisation's activities, and the BCM processes being audited.
- Competencies of auditors.
- Objectivity of auditors (auditors should not audit their own areas of responsibility).
- Document management requirements; though this can easily be incorporated in the overall document management arrangements (*see Chapter 10*).

Management review

The principle behind management review is that the BCMS, in particular the executable parts of it, will be most reliable and useable if it is reviewed for these attributes by management, as opposed to individuals, with clear accountability to the governing body for doing so.

The review process is there to identify changes that are required as a result, for example, of:

- Audits
- Tests and exercises
- 'Whistle-blowing' – discrepancies or inadequacies identified by staff
- Feedback from internal awareness and education activities
- Changes in regulatory or contractual requirements
- Changes in the way that the organisation works
- Changing, or new, good practice, emerging in the business continuity industry
- Changes in policy decided by the governing body.

Ideally, this review will be conducted by the organisation's senior management team, or otherwise, by the oversight body (committee).

Decisions taken as part of the management review should then become actions, or tasks, allocated to responsible individuals, for execution within a specified timescale. These actions should then be monitored and expedited by the senior management team, or the oversight body, as required.

ISO22301 lists both the inputs for the review process ('...*shall include consideration of:*'), which include the reasons for change listed above, and the outputs, which are as one might expect, and include changes to resource requirements, including financial ones.

The frequency of these management reviews is, as always, a matter for the organisation. Those currently operating other management systems will have established similar management reviews, which should provide a yardstick for frequency.

Otherwise, a sensible, starting point might be to review quarterly, allowing the programme management executive, and others, time to execute actions and tasks. The level and rate of change experienced during the early reviews will then inform the frequency for future review.

CHAPTER 8: IMPROVEMENT

Non-conformity and corrective action

BS25999 made a distinction between corrective and preventative (using the form: preventive) actions, however, ISO22301 only states the requirement for corrective action whenever some non-conformity is discovered, which simply removes the need to decide whether something has gone wrong, or could go wrong.

Consistent with other management system standards, there is a requirement for a system to record, and track, anything that is potentially wrong, and to ensure that both the symptoms (usually corrective action) and root cause (usually preventative action) are addressed.

This is another opportunity for organisations with other management systems in place to integrate BCM with them; a non-conformity system can sensibly be made generic, so that it allows actions to be tracked in respect of non-conformity of any management system, whether it is BCM, information security, quality, or any other.

Documentation

There are two, principal forms of documentation required; a non-conformance report, detailing the individual non-conformance; and some form of register, providing an audit trail of non-conformances, as well as a source of management information for performance evaluation.

Examples of both these documents are in *Appendix 6.*

Naturally, where changes to the BCMS are approved and made, those changes will be traceable through the document management protocols that apply to the individual documents, arrangements and the BCMS as a whole.

Continual improvement

Consistent with other management systems, ISO22301 looks for a systematic approach to improvement of the BCMS, through the identification and execution of corrective actions.

In BS25999 it was quite tricky to work out what, over and above the internal audit, management review and corrective/preventative action process, could be done to satisfy this requirement.

ISO22301 helpfully states the requirement for continual improvement, with the suggestion that processes, such as leadership, planning and performance evaluation, may be used to achieve this aim.

A practical step would be to include continual improvement as a standing item in the agenda, or checklist, for management review, thereby providing evidence that action is regularly being taken to consider how the BCMS and its related arrangements can be continually improved.

CHAPTER 9: BCM CULTURE

As with any set of activities in an organisation, if BCM is seen as someone else's responsibility and is not a part of every-day life, then it is not likely to be understood; nor will it work well when needed.

A key difference between BS25999 and ISO22301 is that the previous Standard required organisations: 'to ensure that BCM becomes a part of its core values and effective management … '. In other words, everybody in the organisation must have some awareness of what BCM is, what it is for, how it works, and what it means for them.

This is really a sound philosophy, and whilst ISO22301 doesn't expressly state the same requirement, by requiring awareness, it should result in the same overall levels of capability.

People in organisations often remain ignorant of activities that they are not directly involved in, and they certainly make assumptions about what would happen if there was an incident. More often than not, these assumptions are wide off the mark, and, should they ever be put to the test, the majority of people agree that it would have been much better had everyone been involved in developing the BCM arrangements.

Making business continuity effective

Again, in BS25999's case, there was also a requirement to evaluate levels of awareness within the organisation; again a logical requirement, because it is obviously too late to start improving awareness when an incident has occurred. Now, in ISO22301's case, it is left to the organisation to decide whether awareness levels should be included as a measurable within the performance evaluation arrangements (*see Chapter 8*).

The process must start at the top. Of course, in most organisations some support and approval at governing body or board level is required, in order to commit resources to a BCM programme; but senior executives leading every part of the organisation must be in a position to both support and disseminate the philosophy, policy and strategies surrounding BCM and, in particular, its value to the organisation.

At the same time, most people absorb information more effectively if they are interested in it, rather than being forced to pay attention. So the way that the BCM philosophy is disseminated should be based upon its value to the organisation; it should be seen as something good, something to be welcomed.

Raising awareness

Again, this will usually start at the top. In order to have approved the programme in the first place, the governing body must have a reasonable understanding of BCM and its benefits to the organisation. Directors and senior executives will be involved in propagating some of this understanding throughout the organisation, and some will have BCM response roles, requiring more detailed knowledge.

It is generally effective to create a fairly standard awareness programme that will provide a good understanding of BCM and its value to the organisation. This can then be augmented by more in-depth education and training for those involved in the development, implementation and use of the BCMS.

Awareness techniques

Most people working in organisations today probably perceive that they are suffering from 'information overload'. They feel that they are constantly being bombarded with e-mails, and other forms of information, which they simply do not have the time to deal with.

Documents about business continuity certainly have their place, but the internal 'Business Continuity Newsletter' may not be the most popular read in the canteen, or on the train home.

A two-page (A4) corporate briefing about BCM is probably optimal in terms of people's willingness to actually read and digest its content. This will, in any event, usually result in a significant level of improvement in most people's understanding of the subject, and, in particular, of what it means for their organisation.

Seminars are a reasonably, popular technique and may well prove to be effective in some settings. A classic pitfall with this approach is that many people feel that, to justify having a seminar, it should last for at least half a day. This will not work, at least in the majority of cases. The bulk of relevant information about BCM can be delivered to groups of people in about an hour and a half, with the option of further sessions if the question and answer session at the end is particularly active.

Another quite effective technique is a simple slideshow using PowerPoint®, or a similar application. The 'story' about BCM can be put across in a show of about a dozen slides, which will take most people something like five minutes to watch.

Some organisations use short video presentations to raise awareness. These often prove more engaging for many, and a lot of relevant information can be conveyed in a very, short space of time.

ISO22301 arrived at about the same time as the emergence of viable corporate e-learning systems. It is not unusual for new starters to be required to complete some compulsory training, and equally, e-learning systems being implemented for existing staff can include modules on a variety of core subjects, of which BCM will ideally be one.

Ownership

Even the most experienced business continuity practitioner is unlikely to know the very, best way for a particular activity to be recovered in the event of an interruption. If the owner of an activity makes a positive contribution to the plans for recovery, using their knowledge and experience, not only will the plan be a better one, but that owner is much more likely to both understand and support it.

Of course, people being people, some engage in the BCM programme willingly, and others have to be dragged in, kicking and screaming. It may, therefore, be a good idea to consider integrating BCM responsibilities into the organisation's performance management system or processes. This may include references in job descriptions, with BCM tasks and activities being a regular item for review in whatever performance appraisal system is in place.

It should also be recognised that it takes time, in most organisations, for a new discipline to be understood and accepted. The standard does not require ownership as such, but the evidence that BCM has become embedded in the organisation's culture is much more likely to be convincing if it can be achieved.

Competitive advantage

In many organisations, particularly commercial ones, competitive advantage is likely to be a driver – one of the reasons for embarking upon a BCM programme in the first place.

But competitive advantage can also become a tool in getting the BCM discipline embedded in the culture, simply because it can become part of the organisation's selling proposition; something of which the organisation's people can be proud.

A number of organisations have seen this work to good effect when implementing other management systems with visible benchmark standards, such as ISO9000, ISO27001 and ISO14001.

An important message in the internal awareness building and education programme is that achievement of certification under ISO22301 will be an important component in the organisation's competitive edge.

CHAPTER 10: DOCUMENT MANAGEMENT AND CONTROL

Ultimately, a BCMS is comprised largely of documents. The physical, contractual and financial contingencies that support it may not be documents *per se*, but it is usually the case that their availability and specification are defined and assured by documents. These documents must be accurate, available and secure.

ISO22301 does not stipulate any standard or protocol for document control, but it does set out the following requirements for BCMS records, which are drawn from those contained in ISO9001.

Whilst the wording of ISO22301 is a little different from that of BS25999, its requirements are effectively the same; that all documents that are part of the BCMS, including documents of external origin, must be:

- Controlled
- Identifiable, and including a revision status
- Protected and retrievable
- Reviewed and updated as necessary, and approved for adequacy prior to issue
- Available at points of use.

In addition, the unintended use of obsolete documents must be prevented.

Any document control system that meets the requirements of ISO9001 will also work for an ISO22301 BCMS and, if an organisation already has certification to another management system standard (e.g. ISO9001, ISO27001 or

ISO14001), the document control system developed for that standard should simply be extended to the BCMS.

The international standard for document management, ISO15489-1:2001 Information and Documentation – Records Management, sets out some required characteristics for documents. They must possess:

- **Authenticity** – that the record (document) is actually what it purports to be, and that measures are in place to prevent any unauthorised changes.
- **Reliability** – that the document can be trusted; in this case, to bring about the desired results.
- **Integrity** – similar to authenticity, but includes the requirement that unauthorised changes are visible and traceable.
- **Usability** – simply that the document can be found, retrieved and used as intended; with the important addition of contextual linkages.

This last point is key for BCM documents. For example, where a plan refers to a procedure, it should also identify what that document is, and where it is to be found.

However, ISO15489 does go on to deal with classification of documents; how they are named, and so on, which ISO22301 does not. Many people embarking on a management system for the first time may find it challenging to decide on a system for organising documents. ISO15489 includes a section on the capture of records, which, itself, includes the requirement for 'classification and indexing which allow appropriate linking, grouping, permissions and retrieval, disposition, and identifying vital records'.

Once again, how it is best done depends entirely upon the nature of the organisation in question. Given the likely urgency at the time these documents are needed, a simple system that makes very obvious what each document is and what it is for, would seem to be the best approach.

Reliability

Clearly, the point about the reliability of BCM documentation is that, when needed, the plans, procedures and contact information that will enable the organisation to recover its critical activities as intended, must be complete, and contain the correct information. So, whilst maintaining a comprehensive audit trail of document versions and revision information is useful, it is unlikely to be of very much use at the time of invocation, when key information in a document is missing, wrong, or out of date.

The maintenance and review processes described in *Chapter 8* play a vital role in ensuring that, however comprehensive the document management and control system may be, only the correct version of a given document is available to the command structure at the time of activation.

It is also relatively easy to see how authenticity and integrity can be woven into a document system that assures reliability.

Usability

In practice, review, audit and exercising should lead to the continuous improvement of documents in terms of their usability; in the context of BCM, however, the distribution of documents to authorised holders is an important issue.

With the greatly increased use of electronic media for holding information, it is now more difficult for coordinators to ensure that authorised holders have only the correct version of documents in their possession.

The solutions for distributing business continuity plans and related information to the people who are likely to need them range from hard copy, through exchangeable digital media, to remotely hosted websites. Whatever solutions are selected, their reliability should be included in monitoring, auditing, reviewing and exercising activities.

Some organisations may already use an enterprise-level document management system which is likely to deliver many of the Standard's requirements. Elsewhere, though, the use of conventional document management may be enhanced with some fairly simple standards for BCM documents.

It should be remembered that business continuity plans are likely to be needed without notice, and that hard copies remain the most popular choice of format for many. Where feasible, it therefore makes sense to maintain at least one hard copy of the complete, executable BCMS documentation, in a location where it is most likely to be accessible in the event of a range of major incidents and scenarios.

Templates

Not only will templates provide a consistent and familiar format, they can also create a reasonable level of discipline, in terms of complying with the chosen document control system.

Typically, document templates will include the following:

- Version – *see Version control, below*
- Date created
- Date issued
- Valid until – this should be synchronised with the BCMS review policy (*see Chapter 8*)
- Authorised status.

Inclusion of this basic information on the face of each document should normally provide adequate opportunity for its users to confirm that they are looking at the correct version of the document.

Examples of BCMS document templates are to be found in *Appendix 6*.

Version control

This is arguably the most important aspect of document management, simply because it should ensure that, at the time of use, the correct versions of documents are being employed.

In the absence of a specific document management application, a sensible approach may be to keep all executable BCMS documentation in one place, under the control of a document register or control sheet.

The document register should list all documents in whatever classification system has been chosen, together with data that enables users to verify that they are using the correct version. This form of cross-referencing with the documents themselves should provide adequate assurance, in the majority of cases, that the document is authentic and reliable – key attributes as described earlier in this chapter. *Appendix 7* contains an example of a document register.

There should also be some guidelines, or a procedure, for version control. It is usually counter-productive to produce a new version of a document for something like a punctuation change, yet it will be important that any substantive change leads to the creation of a new version.

A very common problem with using a simple, folder-based system, is that numerous copies of the same document begin to build up, and it then becomes increasingly difficult to locate the correct version.

So, as well as creating the repositories for the current version(s) of documents, it is also a good idea to create archive repositories, so that people are more inclined to remove them from the 'live' folder, rather than deleting them.

Document history

As we have seen, there is very limited value, at the time of a major incident, in being able to look at the history of documents in order, perhaps, to work out why the one in use seems to be wrong, or why a document is missing.

There is, though, an important link between the document history and corporate governance. If things do not go according to plan, there is likely to be some form of investigation. Even when an organisation has followed its own plan, it may well be critical that the way in which the plan was arrived at can be seen. Moreover, it can often be necessary, during the review and updating of documents, to be able to see, and understand, how plans and other arrangements have evolved; for example, a risk control may have been tried before. Knowing who changed what, and when, is very often essential.

Security

There are a few organisations that make their BCP available on the Internet. That certainly helps availability, but, for the vast majority of organisations, this would be unacceptable.

At the other end of the scale, there are BCPs that, of necessity, contain some very sensitive information that simply must not fall into the wrong hands.

Most managers and executives charged with BCM responsibilities will know how to keep their information secure. At the same time, given the importance of availability, care should be taken to ensure that these security measures are not onerous. It may be more appropriate to remove some sensitive information from BCM documentation, for example, instead indicating where that information may be obtained.

CHAPTER 11: REPORTING AND ASSURANCE

Corporate governance

The buck stops, legally, with directors or governors. They are responsible, whether they like it or not, for ensuring that their organisation's risks are appropriately managed.

But, in the majority of cases, members of the governing body are unlikely to routinely ask how the BCM programme is coming on, or whether all the documents due for review that month have been reviewed.

Directors of limited companies generally feel that they are protected from any personal liability if things go wrong. There is an exception to every rule, however, and if those directors choose to ignore the risks of interruption to what their organisation does, then they expose themselves to the risk of being personally liable for any losses that may ensue.

It is, of course, highly unlikely that any reader of this book, or any of their directors, would be in such a position. Directors generally rely on the executive to provide them with the information they need to discharge their duties properly.

Like many other reporting mechanisms in bodies corporate, the executive is expected to provide information to the governing body, so that its members can satisfy themselves that the organisation is being properly run; in this case, that its risks of operational interruption are being appropriately managed.

Including a regular report on BCM in the Board's reporting arrangements, is also likely to help it to become embedded in the organisation's culture – certainly, it will not detract from it.

Those familiar with other management systems will also be familiar with the business of reporting to their governing body. Certification under ISO22301 does provide something of a short cut for the executive, in assuring the Board that the organisation has, and is, operating an appropriate management system for managing the risks of operational interruption.

The ongoing reporting of reviews, audits and exercises will maintain this assurance as, indeed, will the successful outcome of surveillance visits made by the certification body.

Supplier assurance

A good organisation will already be conducting some form of supplier assurance in respect of financial viability, quality, and so on. Where critical activities are outsourced to suppliers or providers, a maximum tolerable period of disruption will have been established for those activities, and it will be very important to seek assurance from outsource suppliers that they also have appropriate BCM arrangements in place, not least so that the RTO for whatever they provide can be met.

The status of suppliers in respect of BCM should almost certainly form a part of the corporate governance reporting arrangements.

Many organisations will also benefit from seeking this type of assurance, in respect of supplies other than outsourced activities.

Due diligence

Every organisation is interested in what people think of it. Whether in the public or the private sector, no organisation today is immune to scrutiny in one form or another.

In the commercial world, organisations are more and more interested in how other organisations that they deal with are run. Investors are particularly interested, as they usually have more to lose if things go wrong.

The quality of reporting, and strength of assurance in respect of BCM, is already an important factor in due diligence undertaken by customers, investors and suppliers. Certification under ISO22301 will be a very, powerful tool in this respect, and the comprehensive nature of reporting will also serve to enhance the due diligence process, which can happen at any time.

CHAPTER 12: CERTIFICATION

One could be forgiven for thinking that there is not much point in developing and implementing a BCMS, unless certification is achieved. Certainly, a potential customer or client is more likely to be swayed by an organisation that has been awarded a certificate, than by one that simply claims that its BCMS meets the requirements of ISO22301. In some organisations, the competitiveness and due diligence drivers may not be as important as in others, yet they may still have the assurance that they have developed and implemented a BCMS according to good, or even best, practice.

But for many, certification is worth the relatively small amount of additional effort and cost.

Essentially, the certification body will be assessing two things; that the BCMS is compliant with the Standard, and that it is being implemented and operated correctly; for example, that the management review process is happening, and that documents are being reviewed and updated.

It is very early days for certification under ISO22301; November 2012 marked the official cut-off for certification under BS25999 and, at the time of writing, the transition arrangements are unclear.

Like other management system standards, the certification process is essentially based upon the auditing of the system itself, and then of the organisation's compliance with its own system.

System compliance

Typically, the first audit visit looks at how the BCMS meets the requirements of ISO22301:2012.

Sections 4-10 inclusive, the material parts of the Standard, comprise 38 substantive clauses, comprising something in the region of 270 individual compliance indicators, depending upon one's reading of the Standard. Essentially, the business continuity manager or coordinator needs a thorough understanding of how the BCMS meets all of these requirements, and where the evidence is that supports this.

It is likely that the certification body will want to see at least three months of audit records for the documentation that has been put in place, though, as the Standard is so new, the requirement for evidence of the BCMS being audited may change.

Terms and definitions

ISO22301 differs in some respects from its predecessor, BS25999. ISO22301 has a significant number of terms listed in its section 3 that are not used in the main body of the Standard. Some certification bodies are more particular than others regarding the use of terminology, but there is ultimately no requirement to use all of the terms in section 3 within a BCMS. However, where terms are used that are also listed in section 3, it is important to ensure that their meaning is the same, and where an in 'in-house' term is used, because it makes sense to keep calling a spade, 'a spade', within an organisation, then it may be useful to include a terminology table in the BCMS that correlates in-house terminology with that of the Standard.

Section 4 – Context

Some management system standards are a little obsessive about things like context and 'understanding the organisation', almost as though people running business don't really know what is going on and how everything fits together.

However, the logic of this section of the Standard is that the BC arrangements should be clearly based upon a comprehensive assessment of the organisation and how it works, as opposed to simple intuition.

Some organisations will already have documented all, or most, of their contextual issues in a business plan, or a similar document, and there is no reason why this couldn't simply be referred to by the BCMS; in fact it is more logical and avoids duplication.

At the same time, there will be things that the Standard requires that are not within the business plan, such as a statement of risk appetite.

Essentially, this requirement is for an executive summary of the business and how BCM fits into it.

Some of the more specific, detailed, requirements are:

Risk factors

This information does actually have a useful purpose and should be satisfied by a statement, or list, of threats that are likely to give rise to operational disruption. The list is likely to include the usual suspects, such as:

- Utility failures
- Extremes of weather

- Fire and explosion
- Information system failures
- Pandemic illness.

In addition, factors such as proximity to a sensitive installation, or heavy reliance on supply chains based in less stable regions, might be included.

Risk appetite

This is covered in *Chapter 3*.

The most obvious way of defining risk appetite is in setting the limit(s) of acceptable risk, easily characterised by the position of red, amber and green bands on a risk matrix.

There is no definitive standard for doing this; it is for each organisation to decide where these limits are, and very often they are modified in the light of experience.

Section 3 – Planning

The auditors will be looking for evidence that the BCMS has been developed, and continuously maintained, with the key elements below.

Scope and objectives

The scope should set out clearly which parts of the organisation, which products and services (remember, the Standard continually refers to products and services), and which activities are included, and what the BCMS is there to protect. Objectives should also be clearly stated, so that there is proper justification for implementing the programme, and also so that the programme can ultimately be evaluated against these objectives.

A sensible place to set out scope and objectives is in the Policy (*see Chapter 1*); they should also reflect statutory, regulatory and contractual duties, and any relevant interests of stakeholders.

In addition, the Standard requires that the acceptable level of risk be stated. This, too, should almost certainly be included in the policy, but it must also be remembered that it is not always possible to state the acceptable level of risk at the outset.

Policy

We have already seen what should go into the policy. The Standard also requires that it should:

- Include scope and objectives
- Be approved by top management
- Be communicated to everyone working for the organisation
- Be reviewed regularly, and also when changes occur to the organisation.

Resources

There should be some evidence that the organisation has determined what resources are likely to be needed. Remember that the full extent of resource requirement cannot usually be established at the outset. However, the resources should contain roles and responsibilities for both the command structure and BCM programme management, including the BCM authority and the BCM programme manager.

The Standard does not set out any specifics about financial, and other operational resources, but it makes sense to be able to show that the programme is likely to be sustainable after certification.

Competencies

The principle here is that, if you have not got people with the skills to maintain it, the BCMS is likely to fall into disrepair. A schedule of competencies will be required (*see Chapter 2 and Appendix 2*), with evidence that there has been a training needs analysis for people who are taking on these roles, and that training is conducted, evaluated and documented.

BCM culture

Basically, if BCM does not become almost an every-day part of the organisation's activities, it is much less likely to be effective. This is one of the harder parts of BCM to get right, not least because it depends, to some extent, on the will of everyone in the organisation. There will need to be evidence that there are activities aimed at raising awareness of BCM amongst everyone in the organisation, and educating those who are likely to have a greater level of involvement in developing the BCMS and, of course, in the BCM response to an incident.

Awareness activities should aim, not only to raise awareness, but to enhance and maintain it. The programme needs to be continuous or ongoing. There also needs to be evidence of a system for evaluating the effectiveness of awareness activities. This is yet another example of the management system trait of 'closing the circle'.

Documentation

In addition to the five areas listed above, there are also clear requirements for all the analytical and executable documentation, which will include:

- Business impact analysis
- Risk assessment
- Business continuity strategy
- Incident response structure
- Plans, associated procedures, and so on
- Contact and other resource information.

There are further requirements for documented evidence of exercising, maintenance and review activities, including the preferred corrective and preventative actions. Not only will the existence of these documents be scrutinised, the document control system, or approach, will also be audited.

Section 4 – Implementation and operation

Still looking at how the BCMS meets the requirements of ISO22301, as opposed to how it is actually being implemented, the auditors will be looking for evidence of whether these parts of the Standard listed below have been reflected in the BCMS.

Business impact analysis (BIA)

The BIA will need to identify the activities that support key products and services (remembering that the organisation decides which products and services and, therefore, activities, are in scope), and the impacts arising from the interruption of those activities, over time.

The key elements that will be looked for in the BIA are:

- A method statement – how the BIA has been, and will be, conducted
- Activities
- Time-based impacts
- MTPD (full activity level) and RTO (minimum activity level)
- Minimum activity level
- Priority of activity recovery (recovery timeline)
- Resources requirements, including outsource providers
- BCM supplier assurance for outsourced critical activities.

Risk assessment

The existence of a risk register, as described in Chapter 3, should form a substantive part of the evidence for this section. In addition, evidence of the following should be made available:

- A method statement – how the risk assessment has been, and will be, conducted
- Impact assessment criteria
- Risk controls or treatments.

12: Certification

Strategy

Much of this will be set out in recovery plans (*see Chapter 5*), though the response structure (command structure) and plans for managing relationships with stakeholders and recovery service providers, may well be set out in other planning components, such as the master plan, scenario plans or procedures.

Because of the structure of the Standard, it is a good idea to create a BCM strategy document outlining the major recovery strategies referred to in *Chapter 5*; so that the auditors can see that the approach to the recovery of activities was established before the response (recovery) plans were developed.

The BCM response

The auditors will look for evidence that executable components in the BCMS are based upon the outputs of the BIA, risk assessment and strategy.

Some of the certification requirements in this section are repeated elsewhere, but evidence will be required of the mechanism for confirming the nature of an incident, activating the response, accessing plans and resources, and communicating internally and externally.

All these requirements can be readily satisfied by well-written plan documents, and a capable, knowledgeable and rehearsed, command structure.

The standard sets out a fair amount of detail in terms of plans, all of it good common sense and not requiring interpretation here. Suffice it to say that the auditors will need to be able to see that plans are based upon policy, strategy, BIA and risk assessment. These requirements also extend to procedural detail, which should be satisfied if the logical and contextual links between documents are correct.

Sections 5 and 6 – Monitoring, exercising, maintaining and reviewing

The Standard's requirements in this area should be substantively satisfied by the existence of:

- An oversight and review body (committee)
- A documented management review process
- A documented internal audit procedure and system
- Maintenance arrangements – essentially the programmed review of documents and other resources
- A system of raising and processing preventative and corrective actions
- An exercise programme – documented records of any exercises conducted will be required for the implementation audit.

BCMS implementation

Having satisfied themselves during the first audit that the BCMS itself meets the requirements of ISO22301, auditors will look, in the second audit, to check how well the BCMS is being implemented and used.

It should also be remembered that there may be some non-conformances identified in the first audit, for which the assessor may allow corrective action to be taken, allowing the implementation audit to proceed. In this case, there may well be the need for a considerable amount of work between the two audits.

Section 3 – Planning

Some parts of this section are not truly implementable, but the auditors will look for evidence that, *inter alia*:

- The governing body discusses BCM, and demonstrates a commitment to it
- The BCM policy has been approved and promulgated
- Roles have been filled
- Competencies have been identified
- Training needs have been analysed
- Training has been arranged, with some having been delivered
- BCM awareness and education activities are making an impact
- The document management arrangements and controls are being implemented; and there are no non-conformities with these arrangements.

Section 4 – Implementation and operation

This should be straightforward, yet can be time-consuming.

The auditors will be looking to see how well the developed BCMS has been implemented, and, in theory at least, should not need to refer to the Standard at all.

So, to be successful in this final audit, it will be essential that all the parts of the system have been implemented, and are being operated as much as possible.

The vast majority of assessors really want the organisation to be successful. If experiences with other management systems are anything to go by, they will allow leeway in certain cases where they can see that there has not been enough time to operate every single facet of the system, and where corrective actions are, for example, possible overnight, for reassessment the next day.

Certification

When the certification audit process has been successfully carried out, the lead auditor will normally make a recommendation to the certification body's certification team, who will make the award.

Naturally, the process does not stop there. There will then be further, continual assessment visits, usually annually, to make sure that the BCMS continues to meet the requirements of the Standard, and reflects any changes to the organisation, and that it continues to be implemented properly.

Keeping documents up to date, executing audits and reviews according to the forward plan, and formally reviewing the BCMS at management level, will all be scrutinised during surveillance visits. Whilst the majority of certification bodies are reluctant to remove certification status, remember that it is within their power to do so.

Any problems identified during these visits can usually be dealt with by corrective action, but, in some cases, this may require a return visit by the auditors to verify what has been done.

Certification bodies

In theory, it does not matter which certification body is used, providing they are UKAS (United Kingdom Accreditation Service) accredited. At the time of writing, the transition from certification under BS25999 to

ISO22301 is a little unclear, and whilst certification appears to be available from some certification bodies, the UKAS website indicates that BS25999 remains available for certification until 31 May 2014.

UKAS has the right to decide who can provide certification because it operates under a memorandum of understanding (MoU) with the UK Government, through the Secretary of State for Innovation, Universities and Skills.

UKAS has also set out some requirements for the re-assessment (at the end of an existing three year certification term) of organisations registered under BS25999-2, by way of transition to ISO22301.

Rogue traders

There are a considerable number of certification bodies which are not UKAS accredited. It is not illegal for anyone to offer, and provide, certification against standards, but it will be self-evident to most that non-accredited certification by 'Tom, Dick or Harry', is probably not worth a great deal – particularly if their consultants have also been responsible for designing and implementing the BCMS in the first place.

It is also theoretically possible that a certification body who, whilst accredited by UKAS for certain other standards, will offer certification under ISO22301. This is most unlikely, but nonetheless, any organisation seeking certification under ISO22301 should satisfy itself that its certification body is, in fact, accredited by UKAS, for this particular standard.

CHAPTER 13: STANDARDS AND CODES OF PRACTICE

In the business continuity world, there are all sorts of references made to various standards, primarily by way of reasons to 'do' BCM.

This short chapter aims to set some of these standards in context, and to explain what the true relevance of each is.

The Combined Code on Corporate Governance (UK)

The Financial Services Authority's (FSA) listing rules,[1] which govern how listed companies should conduct various aspects of their affairs, refers to the Combined Code on Corporate Governance[2] (the Combined Code), which was updated in 2006 and is issued by the Financial Reporting Council.

LR (listing rule) 9.8.6(5) requires listed companies to include, in their annual report, a statement of how they have applied the principles set out in Section 1 of the Combined Code.

For full details, go to the FSA website at http://fsahandbook.info/FSA/html/handbook/D85.

---

[1] The listing rules are part of the Financial Services Authority's Handbook which sets out all of its procedures and rules. The FSA is an independent regulator with statutory powers under the Financial Services and Markets Act 2000.

[2] The Combined Code on Corporate Governance was first introduced in 2003, and was reissued in 2006 by the Financial Reporting Council, the UK's independent regulator for corporate reporting and governance.

Section C.2.1 of the Combined Code requires boards of listed companies to conduct a review of the effectiveness of internal controls, including risk management systems. It further suggests the Turnbull Guidance as an effective means of applying this section.

Turnbull

The Turnbull Guidance on Internal Control is about a wide range of governance issues, and suggests that the system of internal control should enable the company, or group, to respond appropriately to its operational risks, *inter alia*.

So there is a clear, though implicit, regulatory requirement for listed companies to have an appropriate system in place for managing operational risks which, by definition, includes the risks of business interruption.

Sarbanes-Oxley

The Sarbanes-Oxley Act of 2002, issued by the Securities Exchange Commission of the United States of America, governs certain aspects of how listed companies in the United States conduct their affairs. It is predominantly connected with accounting, and the disclosure of financial information, in a similar way to the UK's Listing Rules, and requires these companies to assess their internal control structure. It also requires them to disclose to the public on a 'rapid and current' basis, material changes in operations. Details at www.openpages.com/solutions/sarbanes-oxley/sarbanes-oxley-definitions.asp.

Clearly, this is only relevant to companies listed in the United States, or their subsidiaries, and it is significantly focused on financial information and performance. All the same, it does require these companies to have a system of internal controls, and, as a result, they have to measure and manage their risks (*see Bibliography, Morrison, 2004*).

As in the UK, these include, by definition, the risks of operational interruption that have a material impact upon performance.

Basel II

The Basel Accord,[3] effectively a code of conduct for banks that operate internationally, is almost exclusively to do with financial risk. Whilst the Accord refers to this as 'operational' risk, it clearly does not fall within the scope of operational risk for BCM purposes, and can be ignored, as far as BCM is concerned.

ISO27031

ISO27031 formally replaces BS25777:2008

Information and communications technology continuity management. Code of practice.

A cynical view is that this is simply another version of ISO22301, but badged as part of the 27000 family, to make it appear necessary.

---

[3] The Basel Accord (Basel II) is issued by the Basel Committee on Banking Supervision which comprises banking representatives from a number of European countries, Japan, Canada and the United States of America. The committee's secretariat is based at the Bank for International Settlements in Basel, Switzerland.

It is based upon a number of principles which are both common sense, especially for IT professionals, and generally the same as ISO22301.

When it comes to ICT readiness performance criteria (which ENISA has declared are inconsistent on an international footing), this standard simply says that the organisation should define criteria – not especially helpful!

ISO27001

ISO/IEC 27001:2005 is the international standard for information security management systems (ISMS). It includes limited references to BCM in Section 14 of Appendix A, which lists a total of 133 security controls. Section 14 contains five such controls, which effectively state that the organisations should have plans that address the information security aspects of business continuity; this requirement is entirely consistent with ISO22301.

This means that organisations which are not implementing an ISMS do not need to refer specifically to ISO27001 in order to meet the requirements of ISO22301; while those which are implementing one, need have no fear of conflict between the two standards.

BIBLIOGRAPHY

BS ISO22301:2012 Societal security – Business continuity management systems – Requirements, BSI Standards Limited, United Kingdom (May 2012).

BS25999-1:2006 Business continuity management Part 1: Code of practice, The British Standards Institution, United Kingdom (November 2006).

BS25999-2:2006 Business continuity management Part 2: Specification, The British Standards Institution, United Kingdom (November 2007).

PAS56:2003 Guide to Business continuity management, ISO/IEC27001:2005, The British Standards Institution, United Kingdom (March 2003).

Fire Statistics, Department for Communities and Local Government, London (March 2007).

BS ISO15489-1:2001 Information and documentation – Records management – Part 1: General, The British Standards Institution, United Kingdom (October 2001).

The Financial Services Authority, Full Handbook – Listing Prospectus & Disclosure – Listing Rules, FSA website, http://fsahandbook.info/FSA/html/handbook/D85 (accessed March 2008).

The Combined Code on Corporate Governance, The Financial Reporting Council, London (June 2006).

Sarbanes-Oxley, Corporate Governance and Operational Risk, Morrison, Alan D, Saïd Business School, University of Oxford (2004).

Bibliography

ISO/IEC 27031:2011(E) *Information technology – Security techniques – Guidelines for information and communication technology readiness for business continuity*, ISO, Switzerland, (March 2011).

APPENDIX 1: A BCM POLICY

Business continuity policy

Policy statement

The Board of International Services recognises that the changing nature of the environment in which we operate means that our ability to continue operation uninterrupted can no longer be assured. Whilst we may not have experienced a significant interruptive incident in the past, we know from the experiences of others that International Services also could be seriously affected by an unforeseen incident.

Our customers are entitled to expect that we do everything possible to ensure minimum disruption to our operations, and the delivery of services upon which they rely. To this end, International Services (the company) has embarked upon a business continuity management (BCM) programme which will result in a set of interlocking plans and arrangements that will ensure the best response to a major incident.

The company must be as resilient as possible, so that many incidents outside our control will have little, or no effect, on our operations, and so that, when a major incident occurs, our ability to recover is founded on a planned and well-thought-out approach, utilising contingency resources that we maintain for such eventualities.

In the event of a major incident, priority will be placed upon the safety and welfare of our staff and visitors, above the restoration of business activities. Whilst the two are not mutually exclusive, management focus and resources will be diverted, where necessary, from business activity recovery, to ensuring safety and welfare.

Scope

In order to optimise the application of resources to the BCM programme, the scope defines areas of the company that are subject to its measures and that benefit from its additional protection. These areas are set out in the following table.

Areas of the company falling within the scope of the BCM system	
Locations	Entire head office site, Southampton
	Port operations office, Harwich
	APAC headquarters, Singapore
	Americas headquarters, San Diego
Business units	All business units
Activities	All activities conducted by business units and at locations within this scope
Supply chain	All Level 1 suppliers (ref: approved supplier's list)
Resources	Telecommunications and information systems, including all data in use
	Office buildings and facilities
	Service facilities, plant and equipment
	People

Appendix 1: A BCM Policy

Areas of the company falling within the scope of the BCM system	
Stakeholders	Group board Non-executive directors Shareholders Customers – Groups A and B only
Incidents and scenarios	Any incident leading directly to the prolonged evacuation of the group's facilities Inability to access the International Services corporate IT network Absence due to illness, including pandemic influenza, of significant numbers of staff Political, or other prevention of the delivery of services worldwide
Timeline and phases	The assessment of impact, and planning of response and contingencies, will be based upon elapsed time following the interruption of operational activities, constituting the 'timeline' *The earliest point on the timeline is one day* *The latest point on the timeline is 12 months* The timeline features three phases: 1 Incident response – measured in days 2 Operational continuity – measured in weeks 3 Full recovery – measured in months Plans and contingencies will cover the first two phases: Incident Response and Operational Continuity

The requirements of this policy relate only to the areas of the company listed in the table above.

Appendix 1: A BCM Policy

Business continuity management objectives

The BCM objectives are as follows:

- To ensure the safety and welfare of the company's staff and directors, and of any visitors who are in the company's premises at the time of an incident.
- To minimise the impact on the company of any interruption to normal activities, to a level which is below the impact tolerance level stated in this policy.
- To contain any financial costs associated with interruptions or incidents to levels that will be covered by the company's insurances
- To protect the company's reputation as a reliable and resilient supplier of products and services, and to ensure that business, following any interruption, is not adversely affected by reduced levels of activity during an interruption.
- To protect the company's brand and image in all media, during and following any interruption, so that its ability to secure new business in the future is not prejudiced by the interruption, or the company's response to it.

Business continuity management principles

The BCM system is based upon the principles of ISO22301 (the international standard for business continuity management systems) and includes the following components:

Appendix 1: A BCM Policy

BCM component	Practical requirement(s)
Business impact analysis	Assessment and analysis of the company's operational activities and services, and their relative criticality
Disaster recovery	Arrangements for the restoration or provision of alternative enabling resources, and procedures for the invocation of those resources
BC planning	Documented plans at group, company, division and service levels, setting out key actions to be taken in response to a variety of scenarios, and showing how activities will be restored
Culture	An ongoing programme of activities aimed at maximising the awareness of BCM amongst all staff and stakeholders, and securing collaborative 'buy-in', so as to ensure the continued operability and maintenance of the BCM system
Testing	An ongoing programme of activities that test all aspects of the BCM system, thereby proving its adequacy and operability and providing assurance to the Board

Business impact analysis

The key objective of the BCM programme is the limitation of impacts arising from an incident. However, it is recognised that the company must be prepared to accept a certain level of impact in the event of an interruption, not least so as to limit the level of expenditure on risk controls and resilience measures.

The Board will, from time to time, publish criteria for the assessment of impact. These criteria will include, but not be limited to, impacts whose nature is:

- Financial
- Reputational
- Customer service/satisfaction.

The following table defines the levels of impact that are used in making assessments.

Level	Impact
Very high	Impact that is likely to terminate the group's existence
High	Impact that exceeds the group's tolerance, but from which it would expect to eventually recover
Medium	Major loss of business value
Low	Significant loss of business value
Very low	Minor loss of business value

The company's tolerance level for impact is as follows:

Impact tolerance	Low

Maximum tolerable period of disruption

Generally, the impact sustained following an interruptive incident will continue to increase with time, until the service is resumed. The priority and resource resilience given to each activity is established on an objective basis, so the Maximum Tolerable Period of Disruption (MTPD) is a function of the rate of increase of impact, and the impact tolerance stated above.

Appendix 1: A BCM Policy

For each activity, the MTPD is the point on the timeline at or before which the activity must be resumed, so that the resulting impact will be within the stated impact tolerance.

The recovery time objective (RTO) for each activity is a time period shorter than the MTPD, allowing for the gradual recovery of activities and where the activity can, in any event, be recovered much more quickly. The Board may vary MTPD and RTO at its discretion.

Business continuity plans

In the event of the business continuity plan (BCP) being activated, the command team will use the BCP, and its associated documents, to guide their decisions on response and recovery actions. The structure of plans is as follows:

- Group plan
- Business unit (location) plans.

All plans set out their scope of applicability, so that it is always clear which plans should be activated, and the response and recovery activities that they cover.

Contingencies

The BCM system includes, and relies upon, a range of contingency resources that may be invoked as required, depending upon the nature of any incident.

The arrangements for each contingency resource include a specification for invocation and availability, embodied within the relevant plans and procedures.

Expenditure on contingency resources is based upon the criticality of the activity in question and upon its RTO, and is approved by the Board.

For information and any other rapidly changing resources, a recovery point objective (RPO) will also be established, to ensure that the restored resource provides the appropriate level of operational capability.

Responsibilities

The Chief Executive is responsible and accountable to the Board for the proper development and maintenance of the BCM system.

The risk subcommittee of the Board is responsible for overseeing development, implementation and maintenance of the BCM system, under the day-to-day control of the Group Head of Risk.

All heads of business units are responsible and accountable to the Chief Executive for executing the actions required of them by the BCM Committee and Group Head of Risk.

Approvals of any and all material changes to any part of the BCM system will be approved by the Board(s).

Response organisation

The response organisation comprises the following teams:

Appendix 1: A BCM Policy

Group

The group team is responsible for overall leadership and direction of response activities in more serious cases, and will normally be mobilised in situations where:

- There is a requirement for media handling or public relations
- There are casualties
- More than one site or business unit is directly affected by the incident
- Southampton site is directly affected by the incident.

Business unit

Business unit teams are responsible for leadership of response and recovery activities, and the recovery of activities within specified RTOs.

They are always mobilised when an incident directly affects their operational activities, and they may be mobilised in certain cases when inter-location or inter-unit collaboration or support is required.

Testing and maintenance

The BCM system will be tested on a regular basis, including:

- Desktop rehearsal of business unit business plans at least every 12 months.
- Exercise at business unit level, including testing of in-house and outsourced contingency arrangements at least every 18 months.

- Group-level exercise involving some activation of all business unit plans and testing of in-house and outsourced contingency arrangements at least every 24 months.

A detailed testing plan will be subject to approval annually by the Board, and will be maintained and implemented by the Group Head of Risk.

Awareness and culture

The company recognises that the BCM system will be most effective when all employees and stakeholders have an appropriate level of awareness of resilience, contingencies and response plans.

An awareness and education programme will be developed and implemented by the Group Head of Risk, and the completion of relevant training and execution of actions required to maintain the BCM system, will be treated as objectives within the company's performance management system.

Reporting

The Group Head of Risk will report to the Board on a regular basis that, through appropriate testing of the BCM system and fulfilment of all maintenance actions in respect of plans and contingencies, the company's business interruption risks are being appropriately and effectively managed.

APPENDIX 2: BCM COMPETENCIES

The BCI publishes 10 standards of professional competence for BCM practitioners which are set out in detail in a 38-page document. Meeting these standards is not required by ISO22301, and a more pragmatic schedule of competencies might be as in the following table.

Role/activity	Required competencies
Programme management	Leadership and ability to influence across the organisation
	Project management skills: ability to deliver projects on time and within budget
	Good understanding of all activities conducted by the organisation
	Thorough understanding of BCM principles as enshrined in ISO22301
	Ability to develop and implement management systems
	Internal audit skills
	Document management skills
Policy and strategy development	Strategic (company-wide) planning
	Understanding of financial and non-financial impacts
	Commercial awareness
	Good understanding of manufacturing and related processes
	Good working knowledge of business continuity management principles

Appendix 2: BCM Competencies

Planning and document development	Professional document creation Good understanding of document control principles Ability to understand interdependency with other parts of the company
Document review	Thorough understanding of the process(es) covered Understand of interdependency with other parts of the company Work collaboratively with colleagues to ensure complementarity with other arrangements
Document approval	Strategic (company-wide) planning Understanding of financial and non-financial impacts Commercial awareness Good understanding of manufacturing and related processes
Business impact analysis	Thorough knowledge of the activity in question Good understanding of financial and non-financial impacts Objectivity and impartiality
Contingency planning	Thorough knowledge of the activity in question Good commercial awareness Commercial negotiation ability
BCMS audit	Internal audit skills

Appendix 2: BCM Competencies

Member of the crisis management team	Ability to work as part of a team
	Ability to take effective decisions
	Ability to delegate
	Very good oral and written communication skills
Media spokesperson	Good media handling skills
	Confidence in public speaking
	Good commercial awareness
	Strategic (company-wide) planning
Operational response team leader	Excellent current knowledge and experience of leading the function(s) in question
	Strong leadership
	Effective oral communication skills
Communication cascade group leader	Strong verbal communication skills
	Fluency in English
	Ability to follow written procedures

APPENDIX 3: A RISK REGISTER

| Type | Risk name | Current assessment | | | | Findings |
		Impact	Likelihood	Score	Flag	
Environmental	Severe high temperatures for an extended period	3	1	3		The a/c system cannot cope with ambient temperatures above …
Environmental	Pest infestation	2	1	2		All data cabling is under floor; there was a major rat infestation in …
ICT	Critical failure of file server	3	2	6		The current data back-up frequency is insufficient for …
ICT	Computer virus leading to server failure	3	1	3		Internet security installed may not be sufficient for …
ICT	Critical failure of mail server	2	1	2		The business relies significantly on customer orders by e-mail …
Incident	Fire at night caused by other business tenant	4	2	8		Some tenants in the building operate 24-hrs and there are hazardous materials

Appendix 3: A Risk Register

Type	Risk name	Current assessment			Flag	Findings
		Impact	Likelihood	Score		
Incident	Security evacuation of business park	4	1	4		A secure facility on the business park could be a target …
Incident	Structural failure of building	3	1	3		The business park is built on reclaimed land – no assurance can be provided …
Incident	Lightning strike leading to material damage to the building	5	1	5		There is a higher than average rate of lightning strikes in the area and the building may be susceptible to …
Incident	Flash flood leading to power cut	3	1	3		The electricity substation is in a low gully location, with no effective flood protection …
Incident	Flash flood leading to power cut and evacuation for more than one day	4	1	4		As a consequence of the reclaimed nature of the site and unproven storm water drainage …

Appendix 3: A Risk Register

Type	Risk	Current assessment				Findings
	Risk name	Impact	Likelihood	Score	Flag	
Incident	Denial of access for legal/dispute or similar reason	5	1	5		The premises are in a leased building and the history of landlord changes suggests that...
Resources	Power cut for more than one day	3	2	6		The business cannot operate without electrical power. There is currently no provision for...
Security	Vandalism due to unauthorised entry during 'quiet' periods	5	3	15		The main building entrance is not staffed, and it appears possible for any member of the public to gain access....
Security	Theft of server	4	2	8		The servers are currently in an unsecured part of the premises, adjacent to an unlocked fire exit ...
Security	Theft of back-up data awaiting archive	1	3	3		There is currently no secure storage for back-up data media which is collected for archiving between...

Appendix 3: A Risk Register

Type	Risk		Current assessment				Findings
	Risk name		Impact	Likelihood	Score	Flag	
ICT	Broadband ISP/line failure		3	3	9		The business relies significantly upon e-mail for customer orders. In addition ...
Financial	Insufficient BI insurance cover		3	3	9		The duration of an interruption is unknown. The current limit of liability for loss of profits ...

Risk summary	
HIGH	1
MEDIUM	8
LOW	9
Total	18

Risk score bands		From	To
High		11	25
Medium		5	10
Low		1	4

APPENDIX 4: A CRISIS MANAGEMENT TEAM

This example of a single-level command team may suit 'information processing' type organisations. Others involved in more physical activities would almost certainly require other roles to cover those activities.

Crisis management team	
Role	**Responsibilities**
Leader	Leading the team Ensuring decisions are taken correctly, and in a timely manner Ensuring team members are able to execute their duties and are relieved appropriately
Health and safety and security	Advising the team on health and safety, and security matters Executing immediate incident response, health and safety and security measures Executing the team's decisions on further health and safety and security measures
Human resources	Advising the team on all HR matters Arranging appropriate counselling and other welfare services Coordinating staff communications Arranging agency, or other interim human resources

Appendix 4: A Crisis Management Team

Crisis management team	
Role	**Responsibilities**
ICT	Implementing information and communications technology disaster recovery in accordance with the team's decision(s) Advising the team on all ICT matters Providing and coordinating ongoing additional support for users in interim work situations
Facilities	Managing the immediate response to an incident affecting buildings and facilities Coordinating the deployment of alternative workplace and operating facilities Procuring additional medium-term accommodation as required Planning and co-ordinating return to the premises or new facility projects, as appropriate
Critical activities	Directing and coordinating the resumption of critical or business activities Managing departmental or divisional staff level communications Liaising with HR, and other professionals, in ensuring the welfare of staff

Appendix 4: A Crisis Management Team

Crisis management team	
Role	**Responsibilities**
External communications	Handling all communications with media, including appointing and directing spokespersons Developing relevant media and market statements for reactive and proactive release Advising the team on communications and PR matters Executing other external communications with relevant bodies and stakeholders, including customers or clients
Compliance and standards	Managing communications with any regulatory bodies Advising the team on standards-related issues
Finance	Ensuring the organisation's financial stability is protected Implementing any necessary emergency measures for paying and receiving money Providing necessary financial resources for response and recovery activities
Business continuity	Providing advice, support and coordination to the team on execution of the BCP and its related resources Ensuring the maintenance of appropriate records throughout the activation phase

APPENDIX 5: A COMMUNICATION CASCADE

This is an example of a cascade list that works in practice. Group leaders can see who they need to contact (M = member) and which of them is a leader (L) themselves. If any leader is not available, the details of the deputy leader (D) are also visible. For greater resilience, two or more deputies could be specified (D1, D2, D3, etc.)

First name	Last name	Home phone	Mobile private	Group		
				M	L	D
John	Smith	0208 ...	0773 ...	0	0	
Frank	Jones	0208 ...	0773 ...	0		0
Andy	Langham	0208 ...	0773 ...	0	1	
Charles	Davis	0208 ...	0773 ...	0	2	
Peter	Green	0208 ...	0773 ...	0	3	
Nigel	Taylor	0208 ...	0773 ...	0		3
George	Thomas	0208 ...	0773 ...	1		1
Marion	Turner	0208 ...	0773 ...	1	11	
Louise	Kaye	0208 ...	0773 ...	1	12	
Graham	Irish	0208 ...	0773 ...	1		
Tania	McDonald	0208 ...	0773 ...	1	13	
Bruce	Salmon	0208 ...	0773 ...	2		2

Appendix 5: A Communication Cascade

Linda	Timms	0208 ...	0773 ...	2		
Hugo	Blair	0208 ...	0773 ...	2		
Greg	Soloman	0208 ...	0773 ...	2		
Inderjit	Singh	0208 ...	0773 ...	2		
Oscar	Peters	0208 ...	0773 ...	2		
Nigel	Taylor	0208 ...	0773 ...	3		
David	Maxwell	0208 ...	0773 ...	3		
Craig	Drummond	0208 ...	0773 ...	3		
Paul	Travis	0208 ...	0773 ...	3		
Hugh	O'Driscoll	0208 ...	0773 ...	3		
Gail	Jackson	0208 ...	0773 ...	3		
Philip	Jones	0208 ...	0773 ...	11		11
Helen	Sharman	0208 ...	0773 ...	11	111	
Fiona	Binns	0208 ...	0773 ...	11		
Jack	Rolfe	0208 ...	0773 ...	11	112	
Vita	Franks	0208 ...	0773 ...	11		
Graham	Thomas	0208 ...	0773 ...	12		12
Mike	Kelly	0208 ...	0773 ...	12		
Damian	Fisher	0208 ...	0773 ...	12		
Paula	Gomez	0208 ...	0773 ...	12		

Appendix 5: A Communication Cascade

Frank	Denton	0208 ...	0773 ...	111		111
Harry	Ross	0208 ...	0773 ...	111		
Fabien	de Claire	0208 ...	0773 ...	111		
Louise	Hammond	0208 ...	0773 ...	111		
Ray	Harris	0208 ...	0773 ...	112		112
Colin	Black	0208 ...	0773 ...	112		
James	Hartley	0208 ...	0773 ...	112		
Robert	Plant	0208 ...	0773 ...	112		

APPENDIX 6: DOCUMENT TEMPLATES

PROCEDURE

Document control and change record					
Version	Date created	Date issued	Status/ changes	Editor	Approved
1.0					
No.	P1.01	Title		Owner	

Procedure text:

ACTIVITY RECOVERY PLAN

Document control and change record					
Version	Date created	Date issued	Status/ changes	Editor	Approved
No.		Owner		Valid until	
Activity				RTO	

When and how to use this plan

This activity recovery plan may be used at any time when operations are prevented, due to an incident or situation that prevents normal operations.

The activity should be recovered to a minimum acceptable level, within the recovery time objective (RTO) stated above.

Minimum acceptable level of activity

At or before the RTO (elapsed time following the interruption of activity), the following minimum levels of operational activity are required:

(quantitative description of activity)

The minimum resources required for this service level are:

	Seats	
Office/admin	Terminals	
	PCs	
	Printers	
	Telephones	
Operations/ services	Plant and equipment	
	Services	
	Consumables	
	People	

When the minimum acceptable level of activity has been restored, this must be reported to the Crisis Management Team.

1.0   Loss of premises

In the event that the normal workspace is not available beyond the RTO for the activity, relevant staff will relocate to:

Contact information for gaining access to the workspace:

Contact information for IT network access:

Contact information for general office service provision:

Any significant operational problems that prevent the activity being restored within the specified RTO must be reported to the Crisis Management Team contact.

Other resources must not be used without approval from the Crisis Management Team, as this may prejudice the recovery of other services and have a significant knock-on effect.

Depending upon the nature of the incident or activity interruption, it may be necessary to continue operating in this interim arrangement for up to six months.

2.0   Loss of IT network or applications

2.1   No denial of access to normal workspace

Failure of the entire IT network

The following working arrangements will be implemented:

Failure of required IT applications

Report loss of applications listed in the table below to:

If the IT network is still operational, applications will be restored within the RTO stated in this table:

Application	RTO	RPO

2.2 *Remote access (from home or other workspace)*

Remote access to the IT network is/is not available to this activity.

Procedure to deal with remote network access problems:

3.0 Loss of staff

Significant numbers of staff may be absent for an extended period for reasons which may include:

Pandemic flu

Major casualty count following a serious incident

Security cordon, or other access restriction, requiring most people to remain at home

In the event that more than .... staff are absent for a period likely to exceed .... days/weeks, the following interim working arrangements are to be implemented:

3.1 *Remaining staff operating in normal workspace*

3.2 *Some staff working at home*

4.0 Loss of plant, equipment and services

4.1 *Outline arrangements for:*

Alternative processing facilities

Converting plant and equipment

Subcontracting/outsourcing

Appendix 6: Document Templates

Non-conformance report template
(insert Non-conformance report template)

Non-conformance report register
(insert Non-conformance report register)

APPENDIX 7: A DOCUMENT REGISTER

This simple register, if correctly populated and maintained, should help to ensure that only the correct versions of documents are made available at the point of use.

Category	Section	No.	Title	Issue date	Current version
Policy and strategy	Policy	P1	BCM policy	23/11/07	1.6
	Strategy	S01	Major scenarios strategy	12/02/08	1.2
		S02	Resource failure strategy	01/03/08	1.1
		S03	Political incident strategy	24/09/07	1.5
Plans	BCP	BCP 01	BCP: Group	13/10/07	1.3
		BCP 02	BCP: HQ	27/11/07	1.2
		BCP 03	BCP: manufacturing div.	08/08/07	1.4
	BCP	BCP 04	BCP: regional depots	14/02/07	1.7

Appendix 7: A Document Register

Category	Section	No.	Title	Issue date	Current version
		RP 01	Recovery plan: commercial	12/3/08	1.2
	RP	RP 02	Recovery plan: R&D	01/02/08	1.3
		RP 03	Recovery plan+...		
	Incident response				
Procedures	Resource invocation				

APPENDIX 8: ACRONYMS AND ABBREVIATIONS

Acronym	Definition
BaU	Business as usual
BC	Business continuity
BCI	Business Continuity Institute
BCM	Business continuity management
BCMS	Business continuity management system
BCP	Business continuity plan
BIA	Business impact analysis
BSI	British Standards Institution
CBRN	Chemical, biological, radiological and nuclear
DR	Disaster recovery
FSA	Financial Services Authority
H&S	Health and safety
HR	Human resources
ICT	Information communications technology
ISMS	Information security management systems
IT	Information technology
ITDR	Information technology disaster recovery

Appendix 8: Acronyms and Abbreviations

KPI	Key performance indicator
LAN	Local area network
LR	Listing rule
MoU	Memorandum of understanding
MTPD	Maximum tolerable period of disruption
PAS56	Publicly Available Specification 56
PDCA	Plan-Do-Check-Act
PR	Public relations
RPO	Recovery point objective
RTO	Recovery time objective
UKAS	United Kingdom Accreditation Service

ITG RESOURCES

IT Governance Ltd sources, creates and delivers products and services to meet the real-world, evolving IT governance needs of today's organisations, directors, managers and practitioners.

The ITG website (*www.itgovernance.co.uk*) is the international one-stop-shop for corporate and IT governance information, advice, guidance, books, tools, training and consultancy.

www.itgovernance.co.uk/iso22301-business-continuity-standard.aspx is the information page on our website for ISO22301 resources.

Other Websites

Books and tools published by IT Governance Publishing (ITGP) are available from all business booksellers and are also immediately available from the following websites:

www.itgovernance.eu is our euro-denominated website which ships from Benelux and has a growing range of books in European languages other than English.

www.itgovernanceusa.com is a US$-based website that delivers the full range of IT Governance products to North America, and ships from within the continental US.

www.itgovernanceasia.com provides a selected range of ITGP products specifically for customers in the Indian sub-continent.

www.itgovernance.asia delivers the full range of ITGP publications, serving countries across Asia Pacific. Shipping from Hong Kong, US dollars, Singapore dollars, Hong Kong dollars, New Zealand dollars and Thai baht are all accepted through the website.

Toolkits

ITG's unique range of toolkits includes the IT Governance Framework Toolkit, which contains all the tools and guidance that you will need in order to develop and implement an appropriate IT governance framework for your organisation. For a free paper on how to use the proprietary Calder-Moir IT Governance Framework, and for a free trial version of the toolkit, see: *www.itgovernance.co.uk/calder_moir.aspx*.

There is also a wide range of toolkits to simplify implementation of management systems, such as an ISO/IEC 27001 ISMS or an ISO/IEC 22301 BCMS, and these can all be viewed and purchased online at *www.itgovernance.co.uk*.

Training Services

IT Governance offers an extensive portfolio of training courses designed to educate information security, IT governance, risk management and compliance professionals. Our classroom and online training programme will help you develop the skills required to deliver best practice and compliance to your organisation. They will also enhance your career by providing you with industry standard certifications and increased peer recognition. Our range of courses offer a structured learning path from Foundation to Advanced level, in the key topics of Information security, IT governance, business continuity and service management.

ISO22301:2012 is the new international standard for business continuity within organisations and defines the best practice for developing and executing a robust business continuity plan. Our ISO22301 Foundation, Lead Implementer and Lead

Auditor training courses are designed to provide delegates with a comprehensive introduction and guide to the implementation of an ISO22301 management system.

For further information, please review the following webpages:

ISO22301 Certified BCMS Foundation
www.itgovernance.co.uk/shop/p-694.aspx

ISO222301 Certified BCMS Lead Implementer
www.itgovernance.co.uk/shop/p-695.aspx

ISO22301 Certified BCMS Lead Auditor
www.itgovernance.co.uk/shop/p-1264.aspx

Full details of all IT Governance training courses can be found at *www.itgovernance.co.uk/training.aspx*.

Professional Services and Consultancy

The IT Governance Professional Services team can help your organisation to put in place an effective Business Continuity Plan (BCP) based on ISO22301:2012 (ISO22301) – the Business Continuity Management System (BCMS) Standard.

Our expert BCM/ISO22301 consultants will show you how to best employ the PDCA methodology from ISO22301, to proactively detect, and manage, complex risks, and the threats that can lead to disaster.

With our practical advice and support, you can design and implement a structured and controlled BCMS that demonstrates and provides assurance. Should an interruptive incident occur, you will have evidence that you have done everything that you can to both minimise disruption, and continue supplying your products or services, thus protecting your business reputation.

For more information about IT Governance consultancy services for ISO22301, see:

www.itgovernance.co.uk/iso22301-consultancy.aspx.

Publishing Services

IT Governance Publishing (ITGP) is the world's leading IT-GRC publishing imprint that is wholly owned by IT Governance Ltd.

With books and tools covering all IT governance, risk and compliance frameworks, we are the publisher of choice for authors and distributors alike, producing unique and practical publications of the highest quality, in the latest formats available, which readers will find invaluable.

www.itgovernancepublishing.co.uk is the website dedicated to ITGP, enabling both current and future authors, distributors, readers and other interested parties, to have easier access to more information. This allows ITGP website visitors to keep up to date with the latest publications and news.

Newsletter

IT governance is one of the hottest topics in business today, not least because it is also the fastest moving.

You can stay up to date with the latest developments across the whole spectrum of IT governance subject matter, including; risk management, information security, ITIL and IT service management, project governance, compliance and so much more, by subscribing to ITG's core publications and topic alert emails.

Simply visit our subscription centre and select your preferences: *www.itgovernance.co.uk/newsletter.aspx.*

CPSIA information can be obtained at www.ICGtesting.com
Printed in the USA
LVOW01s2105230115

424067LV00003B/159/P